9000679587

'DISCARDED BY
MEAD PUBLIC LIBRARY.

6|90

DO NOT REMOVE CARD FROM POCKET

A

Mead Public Library
Sheboygan, Wisconsin

Each borrower is held responsible for all library
materials drawn on his card and for all fines
accruing on same.

DEMCO

CARROLL & GRAF

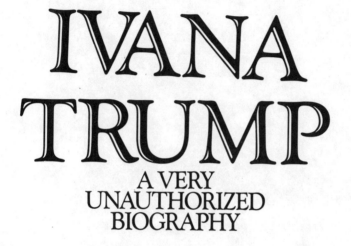

IVANA TRUMP

A VERY
UNAUTHORIZED
BIOGRAPHY

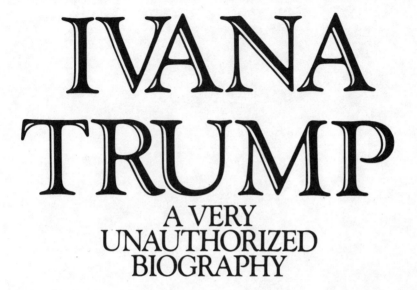

IVANA TRUMP

A VERY UNAUTHORIZED BIOGRAPHY

Norma King

Carroll & Graf Publishers, Inc.
New York

Copyright © 1990 by Carroll & Graf, Inc.
All rights reserved

First Carroll & Graf edition 1990

Carroll & Graf Publishers, Inc.
260 Fifth Avenue
New York, NY 10001

Library of Congress Cataloging-in-Publication Data

King, Norma, 1926–
    Ivana Trump / Norma King.—1st Carroll & Graf ed.
        p.   cm.
    Includes bibliographical references.
    ISBN 0-88184-521-3 : $18.95
        1. Trump, Ivana. 2. Trump, Donald, 1946– . 3. Executives'
wives—United States—Biography. 4. Businessman—United States
—Biography. I. Title.
HC102.5.T79K56   1990
333.33′092—dc20
[B]   90-1696
                                                             CIP

Manufactured in the United States of America

Table of Contents

Chapter One
Imaging Ivana

In January 1989 news surfaced that the name "Ivana" was the subject of an application for a registered United States trademark. This was more than a year before Ivana and Donald Trump revealed their marital problems to a fascinated and goggle-eyed public and quickly became the storm center of one of the greatest media blitzes in history.

Yet, even thirteen months before, "Ivana" could hardly be anyone other than the flamboyant, exciting, and special person Ivana Trump was then and is now.

Ivana Trump was introduced to America slowly and deliberately at first, but her fame escalated so rapidly and energetically in the 1980s that by 1989 she had captivated the minds and imaginations of the public completely. It was obvious that her name did deserve to be trademarked, even in those relatively quiet months before the spectacular 1990 publicity storm when she became what advertising executives deem an "ideal celebrity endorser."

Certainly patenting the name would quite rightly prevent base-metal imitations of her to be thrust upon the marketplace of our culture, and other cultures as well.

Nevertheless, it did not prevent imitators and exploiters from trying. In August 1989 Ivana Trump filed a lawsuit against a discount cosmetic firm for $10 million. The company was selling a line of lipsticks called "Ivana." The real Ivana claimed that the company was invading her privacy and infringing on her trademark—the trademark that had been filed for earlier that year.

"People are using her fame," a Trump lawyer said, "to mislead the trade and the public into believing that [a] Trump has either approved or sponsored the goods. Ivana has been synonymous with the best, regardless of the project or activity. We just don't want people to use her name."

The cosmetic company got the point and ceased and desisted.

There is no one quite like her, nor has there really ever been in the past. And now, after the press circus that attended the Trumps' marital difficulties in 1990, there will be only one Ivana forever. She is a genuine "onliest."

Statuesque, dynamic, outgoing, beautiful in a glamorous modeling sense, fearless, brash, intelligent, energetic, competitive, down-to-earth, self-sufficient, fashion-wise, dominating—all those words have been used to describe this once-in-a-lifetime individual.

So, indeed, have many other words been used just as aptly: tasteless, tawdry, tacky, blowzy, overblown, kitschy, snide, picky, nasty, bitchy.

In spite of this diversity of outlook, Ivana is Ivana is Ivana is Ivana.

The image she projects is startling, eye-catching, spectacular, memorable. It is an image she has perfected through the twists and turns of her adventurous life—from her birth in Gottwaldov, Czechoslovakia, through her emigration to Montreal, Canada, through her marriage and professional life in New York City; Greenwich, Connecticut; and Palm Beach, Florida; to whatever place the solution of her marital difficulties will take her.

The image, like most images, is sometimes confusing, as noted already. But at the time her name was registered for patent, her image was instantly recognizable: the bright red lipstick, the heavy black eyeliner, the wide gum-showing smile, the platinum color,d hair, the slim svelte body, the brilliant crimson nails, the erect athletic posture of a formidable ski-slope contender.

There was, all along, in her interesting, international background, a kind of built-in sophistication that gave her an obvious edge over the untraveled and unworldly people that most of the rest of us are.

So much for the natural advantage this woman possesses through her birthright, her upbringing, and her life story.

Ivana.

First of all, Ivana is the feminine form of Ivan. Ivan is Middle-European Slavic (and Russian) for the name of the fourth biblical apostle, John. Ivana means Joan or Joanne in our spelling. That name, Ivana, belongs to one person only.

Even in appearance, Ivana Trump is a stunning prototype of the truly fashionable world-class billionairess. Once a professional model, as well as a world-class sports participant, she habitually carries herself every inch in celebration of the body perfect.

But there is a great deal more to Ivana Trump than simple good posture.

Actors would call the combination of her natural attributes presence; they are what makes a roomful of people suddenly go dead silent, hesitate as if suspended in time for a long, suspenseful moment, and then collectively let out a long-winded breath in a kind of romantic, susurrant "ahhhh!" to assess the splendorous details of this triumphant apparition.

Ivana, incidentally, may know all the words she speaks aloud in English, but she utters them in the thick, still unaltered rhythms of Mitteleuropa—mixing up the v's and the w's, making the i's into ee's, intuiting with extreme originality her own rhythmic patterns, and maybe coining a few words as well as she goes along.

One somewhat unkind interviewer described her speech patterns as those of a "James Bond villainess." Another spoke of being startled to hear the machine-gun rattle of undecipherable consonant sounds emanating from this completely recognizable and totally American person. Certainly her diction is an international bouillabaisse of words, phrases, and sounds that can charm as well as mystify and confound the average gourmet conversationalist.

But then, it has been often hinted that accents are to actors what trendy clothing is to the rest of us—part of the costume. An intimate of Dr. Henry Kissinger, the guttural and rumbling maven of international politics and secretary of state during the Nixon years, once put it this way:

"When he's not on camera or in public, you don't think he really talks that way, do you? Come on now, in the shower or in the sack, he's just as laid-back and Yankee as the rest of us!"

Similarly, Ivana may not come over so exotic and accented, perhaps, the further away she gets from her public. Of course, we have no proof of this. Donald J. Trump certainly isn't talking. And neither are the other members of her immediate family.

But such speculation is unjustifiable. And her accent and fractured English are so well-known now on television and radio that no one has to try imagining them. Her image has been established and she is frozen into it. All the better that we may see her and believe her to be the Middle-European émigré who made it big by staying exotic.

About her character, there is little mystery or question. She simply exudes a professional competence, self-assurance, and gamesmanship. Also built into her is a fiber of toughness that has only been honed and nurtured in her later years by the life-style she has sought out for herself and which she has led by choice. Strength and resiliency are part and parcel of the character of Ivana. Even in the heat of the Trump triangle, she stood tall and cool, her obvious strength and self-possession dominating not only her husband's rather diffident attitude, but her rival's guilt-ridden distress as well.

Her lifetime interest in and obsession with athletics has given her a firm grip on discipline, has provided her with a sense of what team play means, and, in addition, has allowed her to hone to perfection that most necessary of all talents: the ability to count on yourself.

Work and achieve—but most of all . . . believe.

Not only does she do things, but she does them to perfection.

Nor is there any argument about Ivana's vaunted energy. She has enough for a dozen women—a dozen beautiful women. Sometimes this vast well of churning dynamism causes her to be misunderstood by her detractors. Some, for example, have described her as "steely, tough, and determined," a creation as outrageous and looney as the extravagant ballgowns she wears.

One male reporter wrote that "when you're with her—within full range of her charm and enthusiasm—you're sure she's about to ask you to dance."

Energy in people, however, is not always a plus. Quite a few observers have been overpowered by the energy emanating from Ivana—calling it a kind of hyperkinetic hysteria that flattens out everyone around her.

About the amazing and dynamic duo—Donald and Ivana Trump—the late Malcolm S. Forbes, editor-in-chief of *Forbes* magazine, wrote this tribute:

"Donald Trump's most towering achievement isn't Trump Tower or Trump Casinos or any other of his dazzling great things and doings," Forbes wrote.

"It's Ivana."

And he goes on to elaborate:

"She's not only a mother who sensibly but sensitively dotes on her good kids; she's also a dynamo at the executive desk."

Moving on to describe how she plunged into the work when her husband needed her the most, he says: "In the toughly competitive casino world, she turned a middling one into a triumphant one."

Forbes was writing in 1989, just after Ivana had been made manager of the Plaza Hotel, a brand-new acquisition by her husband.

"Now," Forbes went on, "she's taken up an extraordinary challenge—to make New York's famed old Plaza into a world-class Five Star hotel. Given wage scales of this country's hotel unions and their regulations, that's a daunting undertaking.

"But anyone who knows Ivana can bet she'll get that immensely tough job done, too.

"Besides, she's got a not-so-secret weapon in her armory—The Donald."

But that's an accolade. Witness the brouhaha that erupted just after Donald Trump announced that Ivana would be manager of the Plaza Hotel. Ivana, he joked, would be getting no salary per se, but "a dollar a year and all the clothes she could buy."

Lightning flashed and thunder crackled. None other than Anne Summers, editor in chief of *Ms.*, the magazine of the modern liberated woman, fulminated about Donald Trump's "flippant remarks" concerning the salary offered his wife.

"If [Ivana] wants to be taken seriously as a working woman," Summers asserted, "she should *demand* the going rate as a hotel president—and not accept the dollar and all the dresses she can buy. She has the job—she should get the salary. She can give it away then, if she likes, but she shouldn't *allow* herself to be described in that way!"

Of course, anyone as rich as Ivana and as straightforward is going to make enemies. And Ivana's enemies are legion. Many of them get into print specifically because of their diatribes against her. It is usually in these items that her tastelessness and vulgarity are cited and mused upon.

Typical of the kind of mudslinging that usually occurs was a recent list compiled by Madison Avenue hair stylists. A short list of New York women appeared—including Ivana Trump (with several other well-to-do ladies)—whose hair, the stylists said, looked as if it were "locked in a time warp."

A similar spilling of vitriol in the public prints recently animated Liz Smith, the famed *New York Daily News* gossip columnist, to write a reply to a piece in the *New Republic* that not only compared Donald Trump to Mikhail Gorbachev, but described Ivana Trump as "a vulgar social-climbing wife."

"This is really unfair," Liz Smith snapped back, "because I believe it isn't true. I know Mrs. Trump well and she is anything but vulgar or social climbing. This is a true life partner who has accepted and loves her husband, right or wrong. . . . She wears clothes by Givenchy and Yves St. Laurent, it is true, but they are not vulgar. They are the same clothes worn by other rich women. She is an athlete and a former Olympic ski champion. She speaks at least four languages."

The columnist then went on to point out that Ivana was not interested in climbing the social ladder at all—but was interested almost totally in work.

"You have misjudged both of the Trumps; neither has the slightest idea that they *need* to climb. They are being pursued by the crème de la crème of New York society as if they were the sleigh and society the wolves. Everybody wants the Trumps and everybody invites them and asks them for money for charities because they have money and power. The usual New York high hypocrisy and bullshit is going down all around them, but they don't bother to be a part of it. They have it all. They aren't climbing. They have arrived!"

Even when the chips were down and she was suffering enormous pain over the daily revelations of her husband's extramarital adventures, she hung in there with her usual stolid aplomb. Enough so to inspire accolades:

"She is a decent, caring person and a marvelous mother," said one admirer.

Society's Nina Griscom remarked: "I don't know a lady in New York who doesn't like her."

Real people tend to defy typecasting. It is only the stereotypes that are easy to categorize. At one moment Ivana can be snippish, the next downright nasty, and soon afterward laughing heartily. She can exhibit the most complicated and sophisticated of tastes one minute, and the next display the most garish and bizarre of artistic judgments.

She can be the ice maiden one moment, freezing all within range of her, and she can be warm and friendly the next. She can pierce to the heart some poor middle echelon executive, and turn right around and embrace a low-level worker because she has made an unforgivable error.

In the heat of battle, she can face down a rival who has just demeaned her with derisive comments and stand firm when the ground is giving way under her feet. She can seemingly rise above the petty flaws of her fellow human beings and maintain a supremely cool attitude no matter what her heart is telling her. And when everything is turning against her she can stand firm against the tide and stay calm and cheerful—as she proved to the world in that grim week in February 1990 when her name was as prominent in the press as anyone's has ever been.

Ice maiden? Indomitable queen of all she surveys? Simone Legree with a whip?

There are as many facets to Ivana Trump as there are to the multiple surfaces of a diamond fashioned by a master cutter. There have been highs and lows in her life that almost no one in America can even imagine. She is unpredictable, at some times incorrigible, and always flamboyant.

What are the highs and lows in her life? How did she survive and master them? What is she really like?

Can she even be carefully categorized and rendered into a biographical state?

Chapter Two
Middle Europe

Although Ivana Trump has become one of those so-called household names to the American public, she has never proved to be very cooperative in a public relations sense with those who wish to write about her and seek out her opinion on the myriad of subjects that the media deems fascinating to the American public.

Granted, she does give interviews when something close to her heart is involved—such as the redecoration of the Plaza Hotel, or fund-raising to support one of her favorite charities. She is cooperative, you might say, but in a highly selective way.

In establishing her mind-set about journalism and journalists, Ivana has modeled herself after her husband, Donald John Trump. Jerome Tuccille wrote the first book about Donald Trump, which was published originally in 1985, reprinted subsequently, and then updated in 1987. In his 1987 preface, Tuccille explains how he literally had to turn himself into a detective— read, investigative journalist—in order to get the information he needed to fill in the many gaps in the Trump story.

When Tuccille wrote to Trump, asking for cooperation, he received no answer whatsoever. He then tackled Trump's sister, Elizabeth Trump, and, finally, Donald Trump's mother. After seeing a number of other people in and around the Trump ménage, he was finally contacted indirectly by a "John Baron of the Trump Organization." That is, "John Baron" sought out Tuccille, rather than the other way around. Baron went on the attack immediately, accusing Tuccille of "harassing" the people around Trump, "misrepresenting" himself, and bothering many of Trump's associates.

"You've already been told that Donald doesn't want a book written about him," he scolded Tuccille. And added, rather inappropriately, Tuccille thought: "He doesn't like publicity."

In spite of all this evidence of Trump's feelings about reporters and investigative journalists, the conversation continued, with Baron suddenly reversing his tack.

"I think I can get you an interview with Donald," he said abruptly. Tuccille had written a book about H. L. Hunt, the Texas billionaire, and the Trump Organization had obviously researched it to learn more about Tuccille and his attitude toward the rich and famous. And so Baron suggested that Tuccille send a copy of his previous book—*Kingdom: The Hunt Family of Texas*—and other materials to Trump to establish his credits and qualifications for writing a biography about Trump.

Tuccille did so. His hopes were high. The Hunt book had been well received by the public.

The interview never materialized. Tuccille was forced to go off on his own and research the book without any help whatsoever from the Trump camp.

But then Donald and Ivana Trump both told newspaper sources that they would *not* cooperate with journalists. Too busy? wondered a daily columnist as he churned out his assigned stint on the media-wary Trumps.

It is hoped that this explanation will not only suffice to indicate the number of difficulties encountered in running down hard copy about Ivana Trump, but will also explain why some of the details of Ivana's early life may be a bit equivocal or even totally obscure.

It also may help explain why exact statements cannot be made about certain facts that are usually available to researchers about people in the public eye. In many cases, where contradictory details have distorted the truth, interviews with associates of Ivana Trump have finally set the facts straight, at least within the parameters of human error, exaggeration, or reticence.

In regard to Ivana's early life in Eastern Europe, most of the details have come from personal interviews with associates, and are thus vulnerable to subjective interpretation. These sources are noted.

Even with many of the details on "the early Ivana" shrouded in imprecision, the background and dynamics of her years in Czechoslovakia appear quite clear and unmuddied, in spite of problems of time and distance.

With these facts in mind, it is easier to explore and assess the elements that came to make up her character and personality.

According to one of her interviewers, Glenn Plaskin in the *New*

IVANA TRUMP

York Daily News magazine, Ivana was born on February 20, 1949, in Gottwaldov, Czechoslovakia. She arrived three months premature, and because she was so pitifully small and weak, she was forced to spend the first six months of her life in the hospital.

She was cared for there until August 1949 when she was moved from the Gottwaldov Hospital to her home. Her mother, Maria Zelnickova, a secretary before her marriage, found that she could have no more children. Ivana Zelnickova grew up in a middle-class blue-collar household whose head was Milos Zelnicek, an electrical engineer.

These facts, finally established in the public prints, put to rest various other conflicting details that have always surrounded Ivana's early days. For example, in *Time* magazine on January 16, 1989, she was said to be thirty-eight years of age, which would put her birth date sometime in 1951. In the May 1989 issue of the *Ladies Home Journal*, she was said to be thirty-nine years of age, which would make her birth year 1950. *Spy*'s issue of May 1989 said "it was forty years ago" that she had been born, which would make her birth year 1949. The man who should know—Donald Trump—did not specify *any* year in his book, *Trump: The Art of the Deal*.

Even the place of her birth was uncertain for some time. According to some press releases from the Trump organization, she was born in Vienna, Austria. *People* magazine followed that lead, referring to its December 7, 1989 issue, to her "dual Canadian-Austrian citizenship." However, *Spy* put her birthplace as "possibly in Czechoslovakia." And *Manhattan, Inc* stated flatly that she was born in Prague, Czechoslovakia.

Let's look at her true birthplace now. The town of Gottwaldov was known as Zlin until it was renamed after Klement Gottwald, who served as president of Czechoslovakia after the country was overthrown in a Communist coup in 1948. It was Gottwald who, unhappily, made Czechoslovakia a satellite of the Soviet Union.

Gottwaldov—formerly Zlin—is located some 135 miles east and slightly south of Prague. It is a middle-sized town, by Czech standards, of about 50,000. Gottwaldov was always a company town. The predominant company was the Bata Shoe company, founded in 1913 by Thomas Bata, although other goods made of leather and rubber were produced there, too. Under the Bata family, the town grew into a self-sufficient factory town, with a number of other consumer-goods factories, educational facilities, and model-housing projects. Branches of the Bata Shoe company opened up throughout the world.

When the Communists took over in 1948, all the companies in Gottwaldov-Zlin were nationalized. Members of the Bata family escaped and built shoe factories in South America and Canada.

Ivana's family name—her maiden name as we call it—has been finally established as Zelnickova. The 1984 *Current Biography Yearbook*—in an article about Donald Trump—called her Ivana Winklmayr; later, in Trump press releases, her name became Zelnicek. Jerome Tuccille's biography of Trump called her Ivana Zelnickova Winklmayr.

A bit of explanation is obviously in order. The Czechoslovakian language is inflected—that is, the endings of nouns and adjectives change according to gender and declension. Ivana's father's name is Zelnicek. Her mother's name—and hers—is Zelnickova (the feminine form of Zelnicek). Usually the feminine form simply adds "ova" to the masculine form—but names ending in "cek" are exceptions to the rule. The middle "e" is always dropped when adding the "ova." Thus: Mr. Zelnicek; Mrs. and Mr. Zelnickova.

In a Canadian newspaper story about Ivana, the *Montreal Gazette* (now defunct) printed her name as Ivana Winklmayr-Fielnickova—the last half of the hyphenated surname an obviously erroneous attempt at a phonetic spelling of her name. In Trump's autobiography, which should be the final word, her surname is not mentioned at all; she is simply "Ivana" or "my wife"—clearly a case for the women's liberationists.

The mystery of the Winklmayr element in Ivana's name has finally been cleared up, and will be discussed in detail later in this chapter. Its continual surfacing in Ivana's history has, however, added fuel to the fires of unsubstantiated rumors about her past.

Her mother, Marie (Maria) Zelnickova, was a typically middle-class Middle-European housewife, described as Czechoslovakian in several stories, and Austrian in *Spy*'s expose in May 1989. She was not a Western-oriented woman, with a dream of equal rights, or any professional aspirations. She was, very simply, Ivana's mother, and, as such, tended the home for her husband and daughter.

A note now on the spelling of Maria Zelnickova's name. The

Czechoslovakian spelling of the American Mary—Italian Maria, etc.—is Marie. But since we have adopted the Americanized spelling of most Czech names in this book, Maria Zelnickova (Czech) will appear as Maria Zelnickova (Americanized). The Americanized spelling of such names is usually at the behest of the person carrying the name.

It is possible, of course, that Maria was of Austrian birth. That would account for Ivana's possession of the dual Canadian-Austrian citizenship mentioned in *People*. As a child of Czechoslovakian-Austrian parents, she could have opted for Austrian citizenship when she attained maturity, thus allowing her to leave Czechoslovakia through Austria, which allowed easier emigration to the West. A look at the map of Europe shows how much closer together Vienna, Austria, and Gottwaldov, Czechoslovakia, are than, say, Vienna and Prague.

As for Ivana's father, even his occupation tends to become blurred in the shifts and emendations. *Spy* says flatly that he was an electrical engineer. So does Tuccille. To dilate upon that description a bit by adding a detail of information, its author, Jonathan van Meter, confirms that Milos Zelnicek was a Czechoslovakian citizen. Michael Shnayerson in *Vanity Fair's* January 1989 article, describes Zelnicek as a Czech architect. Margo Hammond, in *McCall's* February 1989 issue, describes him as an engineer and a Czech; engineer in this sense would probably mean civil engineer, hinting at the possibility that he might also have performed services as an architect at one time or another, thus conforming at least partially to *Vanity Fair's* job description. At the time of that writing, Ivana's birthplace was not yet accurately established by researchers.

At this late date, it seems quite logical to assume that Milos Zelnicek was indeed an electrical engineer. In the 1950s, they were still making a lot of shoes in Gottwaldov-Zlin. "Ivana's father was probably working on the machinery." at the shoe factory, Michael Syrovatka, who runs a ski-repair business in Montreal and who knew Ivana in Czechoslovakia, said in an interview recently.

Thus, the true origins of Ivana Zelnickova, if indeed that is her full name, are obfuscated. Because it has become so difficult to piece together information about "Ivana Trump," inaccuracies and second guesses will remain until a definite statement from

Ivana Trump clears up the troubled waters. Secrecy breeds falsity.

Nevertheless, Ivana herself, with her background somewhat inchoate and undefined, is a typical example of Middle Europe in the years just following World War II. In that troubled historical milieu, constant contradictions, unclear allegiances, and dubious political ties were a way of life. When, in Churchill's ringing words, "From Stettin in the Baltic to Trieste in the Adriatic, an Iron Curtain has descended across the Continent."

Now is the proper time to explore the environment in which Ivana was born and brought up. All Czechoslovakia, including Gottwaldov, was in the eye of the postwar storm over Europe—the storm of reaction and repression that was swirling through the area taken over by the Soviets after the end of World War II.

To back up a bit, Czechoslovakia was created in 1918, at the end of World War I, when the Western powers chopped up what was left of Germany, or, actually, the old Austro-Hungarian Empire. That included several ancient states such as Bohemia, Moravia, Ruthenia, Slovakia, and parts of Hungary. Gottwaldov-Zlin lies within the borders of ancient Moravia, not far from the Moravia River. The new state established a so-called democratic system of government, and under Thomas Garrigue Massaryk and Eduard Benes, its first and second presidents, it became a viable Middle-European nation. Nevertheless, it was a nation constantly troubled from within by built-in conflicting nationalistic struggles—mainly involving enmity between the Germans and the Hungarians.

During the following decade, Adolf Hitler played on the disaffection of the German minorities in Czechoslovakia, and eventually engineered the Munich Pact, which, when signed in 1938 by the Western powers, allowed Germany to take over the Bohemian borderland (called the Sudetanland). Czechoslovakia as a nation was doomed to evisceration.

In 1939 Germany dissolved the newly created state of Czechoslovakia, carving "protectorates"—puppet states—out of Moravia and Bohemia, awarding Ruthenia to Hungary, and creating an independent state of Slovakia. These states remained as such during the devastation of World War II, until the area was finally liberated by United States and Soviet forces in 1945.

The German population was then expelled from the country,

and what was left of Czechoslovakia fell under the dictatorship of the Soviets—more or less by the default of the Western powers. A Communist-dominated coalition government ruled, as might be expected, until 1949, when the Soviets took over the country completely and established a Kremlin-controlled puppet state.

During the 1950s and early 1960s, the country was practically dormant, surviving as best it could under Soviet repression. Once the most prosperous and productive area in Europe, containing the great Skoda Works and other giant manufacturing establishments, Czechoslovakia was soon completely nationalized, with management of the companies turned over to the socialist government—as were, of course, the Bata Shoe works. This radical change resulted in eventual inefficiency and a gradual decline in productivity, contributing to economic problems and a much lower standard of living for the nation.

By 1963 there were stirrings of rebellion against the Soviet oppressors, and within five years the Czechs were able to install Ludvik Svoboda as president and Alexander Dubcek as party leader—the same Alexander Dubcek who in November 1989 stood in Wenceslas Square in Prague, and told the assembled multitude of cheering Czechs: "I am among you again!" Both men were liberals who tried to bring a true self-government to the Czechs for a period during the 1960s.

As everyone who has read a newspaper or tuned in a television news program in 1989 is now aware, this period was known as the Prague Spring. Sadly, it was to be short-lived. In August 1968 the Soviets, under Leonid Brezhnev, sent tanks and guns to crush Dubcek's government, stating unequivocally that any country once in the Communist system would never be allowed to change to any other type of government.

It was, to truncate a famous Dickensian construction, "the worst of times." And yet, those months of the Prague Spring were crucial ones for the teenaged Ivana Zelnickova. Ivana had grown up a child of adversity and dissent. The times had made her what she had become. People reared under oppression such as Czechoslovakia's tend to acquire a habit of survival—either that, or they perish. To remain afloat against the crosscurrents of politics, sociology, and hard times that swirled about the world that Ivana inhabited, she found that she must first of all become adept at maneuvering somehow through these stormy waters.

She was involuted naturally, tended to be quiet and very controlled, and in this mode she was well able to take care of herself. Psychologically shrewd, she soon acquired the ability to see through sham and the masks others put on to screen their true motives; she learned to read people well. She was alert mentally, and bright in a way that was almost more masculine than feminine. And, physically, she was attractive—but also, more important, she was strong and quick.

According to one source, her natural beauty made her into a kind of Bohemian Shirley Temple as she grew up. That source says that, in fact, she was so similar to Shirley Temple that she even played roles as a child actress in at least four Czech motion pictures. Meanwhile, in order to realize his fantasies of an heir (instead of an heiress), her father began to train her as a competitive athlete—as if she were the son he did not have.

Milos Zelnicek was a swimming champion. When Ivana was only two years old, he taught her how to swim. But swimming was secondary to Milos Zelnicek's dreams for his daughter.

As soon as she could walk, he strapped his daughter onto midget skis, and taught her how to race down the steep mountainside. She was a skier from then on. By the time she was six years old, her father had put her on the ski circuit, where she became a contender in a number of competitions, winning the very first downhill race she skied in.

According to Donald Trump in his autobiography, "By the age of six she was winning medals." Unfortunately, there is no hard evidence of this fact, either in the medals themselves, or in actual reports of her triumphs.

Whatever, it was during these years that she honed all her competitive skills to a startlingly successful edge. Competition. Exercise. Speed. Building up the muscles and the persona. Learning how to take care of herself. Being always able to survive.

Wartorn Czechoslovakia taught her the need to know how to survive—and to aim toward survival in every step in life she took. One of these survival tactics was not to reveal a great deal about herself or her family. Anyone who has lived in a country like Czechoslovakia under the Soviets acquires a defensive reticence about the people one knows and loves. Ivana did survive. In fact, she survived, and effectively flourished.

Many years later she once tried to explain why she had succeeded so well. "Sports gave me the competitiveness and discipline that have been important to my success," was the way she put it.

"You get certain values," she said. "You follow a program from morning to night. You must do things on your own. There are no parents, there is no tutor, no cook."

She learned self-reliance from her father. "Going down a ski slope at a hundred miles an hour, you have only yourself to count on. Nobody else can do it for you. I learned quickly, and I haven't forgotten those lessons. Discipline. It takes incredible discipline."

But she learned much more from skiing than just self-reliance. Skiing gave her that inherent sense of competition so necessary for participation in the contest of life that is waged constantly in the real world of today.

Besides, growing up in Czechoslovakia, a country under the strict domination of the Soviet Union, was certainly no picnic. It was a place "where nobody ever gives you anything for free—not that anybody ever does anywhere."

But learning to cope with the life style in a dictatorship taught Ivana most of all to develop self-reliance and to depend on herself throughout her life.

"When you're raised in a Communist country," she said, "you lead a very Spartan life. You start with nothing, and you learn that you must work hard for everything and believe in yourself."

By the time she reached the age of twelve—about 1961—her father had enrolled her in a very strict, very demanding, very regimented Communist bloc training camp for child athletes. From then on, she was zooming down the Austrian ski slopes at sixty miles per hour in competition and in simple fun.

For Ivana, athletics was one of the ways she could excel and make her father proud of her. In addition, because Czechoslovakia was Communist-controlled, her superiority in athletics made her one of the favored few in a nation that had few favorites.

She skied and skied and skied; she loved every minute of her athletic life; she thrived on it. Her specialty was the downhill and the giant slalom.

"I was a daredevil," she recalled, "though I was always scared on the downhill and broke my bones a thousand times." In fact, she did break her legs at least five times. "Thank God," she said, "I have no pain."

It was when she was twelve years of age that Ivana Zelnickova learned a lesson that was corollary to her sports training. Up to that time, she thrived on sports, and won races, and was considered an excellent swimmer and skier.

But now her father discovered something about her that did not please him. In school Ivana Zelnickova had become not only an indifferent student, but actually a fairly poor one. Milos Zelnicek was an intelligent man who prided himself on his intellectual resources and achievements, as well as his outdoor sports accomplishments. He knew that somehow he had failed to instill in his daughter the proper traits of character that would make her an intellectual achiever, as well as a physical achiever.

And so for fourteen days, Ivana Zelnickova was forced by her father to spend all her waking hours working inside the shoe factory where he worked. She was put on the assembly line, where she sat for hour after hour, hammering heels onto brogans.

She knew she had been placed there as punishment by her father. She was being taught a lesson for not bothering with her schoolwork. She knew that from the first instant she had been made to hammer on those miserable heels.

"I was petrified," she said, remembering this ordeal many years later. "For I was scared to death that I would wind up doing this one little thing for the rest of my life!"

After two weeks her father relented. Ivana was freed from the assembly line, and she immediately set out to prove to her father that she understood what he had been trying to tell her.

"I promised myself that I was never—*ever*—going to do that kind of work again!"

When she came out of the factory, she hit the books and took to studying with as much avidity as she had taken to her sports activities before.

She was smart. She simply had not applied herself. Now she got her act together and became a much better student than she had ever been before. Her improvement was dramatic enough to impress her father and her mother.

Her father's lesson taught her that she could be good at whatever she set her mind to—intellectual endeavors as well as sports. And after that lesson, she never once looked back. She studied and studied and studied. She had the brains as well as brawn. Her brightness and skill with numbers was obviously a legacy from her father, for whom figures had always been second nature. The lesson in the shoe factory finally opened Ivana's eyes to the fact that she was smart as well as athletically skilled.

More than muscles and skiing skills began to intrigue Ivana now. Her instincts told her that with her looks and athletic skills she could seek out something else—something she now knew she was born for.

The spotlight.

She was smart, she was competitive, she was good-looking in a thoroughly middle-class way: long brown hair, brown eyes, glowing skin tone, a svelte figure. Already she was acquiring a patina of glamour. And the glamour that she acquired was beginning to get—well—results.

She did well in the limelight, where she knew she was fated to be. So well indeed that she attracted the attention of one of the best skiers in Czechoslovakia. Not only was this man one of the best racers, and a member of the country's acclaimed ski team, but he was very good-looking, very competitive—much like Ivana—and very much sought after by the women athletes.

And so George Syrovatka decided that Ivana Zelnickova was probably one of the best female skiers he had ever seen. He was interested in the fact that Ivana not only skied competitively, but swam competitively, too. This put her on a plane slightly above that of the other women he knew.

"George was a very good-looking man, a very successful athlete in Czechoslovakia, from a good family," said Monique Clement, a model in Montreal, Canada, who was later married to him. She continued her description of him as "a nice guy who happened to look good and *be* good in a lot of things."

According to Clement, Syrovatka came from a family that was wealthy and politically prominent. His grandfather had been a government official, but was killed by the Germans during World War II.

Soon the two of them—Ivana Zelnickova and George Syrovatka—were going steady, to use the American phrase. "They were in love," said George's brother Michael. He explained that they would go to all the ski races. "They spent most of their time together." Michael remembered that Ivana was about eighteen at the time. George was about twenty-four. There was a group of skiers that they hung around with—a kind of "jock" crowd of the best. "They'd make parties or go out together."

At times they would go out to George Syrovatka's grandmother's place in the country. She was the widow of the grandfather who had been murdered by the Germans. There they'd drink beer and go swimming together in the pool, and listen to music—the kind of thing young people the world over do in their spare time.

Ivana was in love. So was George. But skiing was only part of George's life. He could not be with Ivana all the time on the slopes. He was a student at Charles University in Prague. In fact, George lived in Prague; Ivana was over a hundred miles away in tiny Gottwaldov. "That would be like George being in New York and Ivana being in Boston—and meeting in Vermont," Michael explained.

There was one solution, and Ivana spotted it immediately. And what Ivana wanted, Ivana got. With a middle-class background, of course, it was not easy for a woman to get a college education. But in Ivana's case, she was an only child. And she had always done everything she could to please her father. Both her parents tended to spoil her. The Zelniceks were reasonably well off and nothing was too good for Ivana.

And so she now advanced a bold idea to her father. She would go to college to get a physical education degree. To do that she would have to move to Prague. After much discussion, it came out exactly the way Ivana had known it would. Her parents agreed.

Quite soon after that, Ivana applied for admission and was accepted. By the late 1960s—it was around 1968—she was enrolled and taking part in a rigorous physical education training.

If there is one thing the Communist countries do, it is to develop their athletes so that they can compete successfully with the athletes of other countries. Sports has always been a cachet in the Warsaw Pact countries. Charles University participated in this sports training, in spite of its historic past and classical background.

Little known in the Western world these days, Charles University, originally called the University of Prague, has a long and honorable history in academic circles. For hundreds of years, it was one of the centers of culture in what was then the nation of Bohemia. The Charles in the name of the university refers to Charles IV, Emperor of the Holy Roman Empire and King of Bohemia. Charles IV lived in the fourteenth century. He was a vigorous supporter of Pope Clement VI and Pope Urban V (the latter the famed Pope at Avignon) in his wars against the powerful French emperor, Louis IV.

In 1348, at the height of his power, the Roman Emperor Charles IV founded the University of Prague, later Charles University. Prague was thus one of the first universities on the European continent. It underwent a meteoric rise in popularity once it opened its doors to the world. Students flocked to this center of learning from all the countries in Europe.

As the university's fame grew, so did Prague itself. From its founding in 1235 by King Wenceslas I (yes, that is the man known today in the famous Christmas song) it had been a small walled city. Under Charles IV's reign, Prague expanded into a new town—a larger one also walled against potential invaders.

It was to this famous historical landmark that young Ivana came to study—and to be with George Syrovatka. Technically, Michael Syrovatka explained, the couple were living separately, but, essentially, "they were living together."

To elucidate, "Ivana was officially living in a dormitory, and George was living at home. But let's say my parents would go away, and she would come over and stay at our house. That's how it worked. I would go with my parents to my grandmother's in the country and George and Ivana would stay in town."

In those happy years at Charles University, Ivana continued to improve her skiing techniques. She never lost sight of the fact that she lived in a Communist-dominated world that accorded its athletes far greater fame than its intellectuals. Yet she pursued her academic work, too—and did well, thanks to her earlier decision never to wind up pounding heels onto brogans in a hot, stuffy shoe factory.

But Ivana certainly did not rest on her educational and skiing laurels throughout her college career. Her energy and initiative drove her into other areas of endeavor. She began seeking modeling jobs and managed to make a satisfactory debut in the business—a definite tribute to her lithe, poised, model-like beauty.

She was featured on the cover of at least one fashion magazine and appeared in inside stories as well. The magazine whose cover she adorned was called *Moda* (Fashion). By the time she took up modeling, she had begun to color her hair blonde; it was naturally dark brown.

An especially elusive rumor about Ivana's life while at Charles University continued to surface later on, but could never be verified. One of her teachers was quoted as saying that she was briefly engaged to a film director. Obviously nothing ever came of the engagement, if it ever took place, and details of the episode proved impossible to substantiate.

Nevertheless, she did appear in a Czech motion picture film titled *Pantau*, made in 1970, definitely during the time she was a student at Charles University. The rumor about her engagement may have come about because of her work on that picture. The details remain obscure.

It was while Ivana was in college that the Prague Spring occurred. During Alexander Dubcek's short regime, the Iron Curtain that cut off Czechoslovakia from the West was more or less breached. Michael Syrovatka and his parents chose that time to emigrate from Czechoslovakia to settle in Montreal, Canada.

"There was a period of a couple of months in 1968 when it was easy to get out," Michael remembered. "That's the time we left. Then they tightened up the borders again, shut everything down. From then on it was fairly hard to get out"—fairly hard, if not downright impossible.

And that meant trouble for Ivana and George. George opted to stay behind with Ivana. He wanted to finish his university course in engineering and graduate with a degree. Ivana, too, was trying to finish her degree. George finally managed to get to Montreal in 1969, but it was only on a visiting visa, and he soon returned to Prague and to Ivana.

By 1971, George had graduated, but Ivana had not. It was almost impossible to get out of the country at that time. The Soviets had installed their own hand-picked man to run the show—a puppet politician named Gustav Husak. The bloodshed of 1968, when Dubcek was ousted, was a bitter memory; but at least things had calmed down again. The rioting had been neutralized, and the students, as well as the civilian population, were put on stern warning.

In 1971 George Syrovatka participated in a ski race in Austria.

He was still a good competitor and well-liked and respected by the Czechs in charge of the national sports program. He simply stayed in Austria after the races were over. Technically, he defected, as many other sportsmen and sportswomen have done, during athletic competitions.

That left Ivana stranded in Czechoslovakia, with George in another country. And now we enter another cloudy region of Ivana's life in which two points become ever more confused.

One concerns an offhand mention of an incident that occurred in Czechoslovakia, and about which there is absolutely no other evidence.

"I had one tragedy in my life," Ivana told *New York Daily News* magazine writer Glenn Plaskin. "I had a boyfriend in Czechoslovakia who died in a car accident, and frankly, that's one reason I came to Canada. I needed to go away, and forget . . . if you ever forget. It took me about five years to be able to talk about it."

Was she in love with this man? Plaskin asked.

"Yes. It sure put things in perspective," she said.

Recently, information published in the London *Daily Mail* revealed—whether true or not—that Ivana was engaged briefly to a Czechoslovakian lyricist named Jiri (George) Staidl. Well-to-do and a success at his profession, Staidl and Ivana were apparently engaged for a short period until Staidl's tragic death in 1973, according to the *Daily Mail*. He was thirty years old at the time. A recent recap of this story in the *New York Post* included a photograph purportedly of Ivana and Staidl.

The second cloudy point involves Ivana's sports accomplishments.

According to Donald Trump's autobiography, "In 1972 [Ivana] was an alternate on the Czechoslovakian ski team at the Sapporo Winter Olympics." Tuccille writes: "Throughout the competition she sat on the sidelines and looked on in frustration as Marie Therese Nadig of Switzerland won the women's downhill, beating the odds-on favorite, Annemarie Proell of Austria."

Spy's researcher, Jonathan van Meter, reports that when he contacted Petr Pomezny, the secretary of the Czech Olympic Committee, he was told that there was no record at all of Ivana on file. "Who is this Ivana woman, and why do people keep calling us about her?" Pomezny asked van Meter. "We have searched so many times and have consulted many, many people, and there is no such girl in our records."

But Aline Franzen writes in "The Non-Stop Ivana" in the May, June, July 1989 *The Best in the World #20* that Ivana "joined the Czech National Ski Team, competing at the 1972 Olympics in Sapporo, Japan, finishing seventh overall." Patricia Lynden reports in the *New York Times* of August 30, 1979, that Ivana "was an Olympic skier in the 1971-1972 Olympics at Sapporo, Japan, ranking seventh overall on the Austrian ski team." Czech ski team? Austrian ski team?

When asked straight out whether Ivana was or was not on the Olympic ski team, Michael Syrovatka replied, "No, she was on the University team."

"But *was* she on the Olympic team?" he was asked again.

"That depends on what you would call Olympic," he said. "I guess you could call it a future Olympic team. She did not go to the Olympics. She never went to the Olympics. She was not on the Czech Olympic team." Or, presumably, on the Austrian Olympic team. "I don't know. She could have been an alternate—that's very ambiguous. But she was not at the Olympics in Sapporo."

She was quite probably at Charles University completing her studies. "She was very much into her sports and into her studies while she was there [in Prague] and very close to her parents," Monique Clement said.

Ivana earned her masters degree in either 1972 or 1973. She knew what her next move would be—if she could make it. Clement agreed that it was the fact that George was in Montreal that prompted Ivana to make a very hard decision in her life. "For her to leave [Czechoslovakia and her parents] was an extremely hard decision to come by."

Yet, in spite of any emotional difficulties, the decision she made was the only logical one possible. The problem was that it was not quite as easily arranged as thought about.

According to Michael Syrovatka, it was George who arranged for Ivana to cross the Iron Curtain and get out of Czechoslovakia. The exact details of her escape were unknown for some time. What was the sequence of Ivana's movements in those post-Prague Spring years? Those steps were as clouded as were other details of her early life.

For example, take an interview that was broadcast in October 1989 when Ivana was questioned by Regis Philbin and Kathie Lee Gifford on ABC-TV's *Regis and Kathie Lee Show*. It affords an example of the kind of difficulties encountered in trying to trace Ivana's actions in 1972-1973.

Philbin was trying to coax out of Ivana some details of her earlier life by showing her some photographs. But he found it was not quite that easy.

"All right, Ivana Trump," he said, starting out with confidence. "This is your life! Anyway, let's start from the beginning and let's find out a little bit about you. Now, there you are," he said, holding up a picture of Ivana. "Could be anybody's daughter right there."

"Is that in Czechoslovakia, Ivana?" Kathie asked curiously.

"Yes, it is."

"Now, how long did you stay there?" Regis asked.

"How long I was there?" Ivana pondered. "About fifteen years."

Philbin repeated the number of years, and Kathie asked, "Emigrated to—?"

"Went to Vienna through Czechoslovakia back and forth," Ivana said. And just how did Vienna get in there? Was it part of the escape route to the West?

"Oh," Kathie repeated, puzzled. "To Vienna and *then* on to Canada?"

Ivana seemed to want to get it straight once and for all. "From Vienna to Czechoslovakia and then to Canada, yes." Let's see, born in Gottwaldov, traveled to Vienna, and then on to Canada. Right?

"And in Canada then, in your teen years, right?" Fifteen years in Czechoslovakia, Kathie was obviously thinking, meant Ivana was still a teenager when she got to Canada—if, of course, she was slicing off a few years just for good measure.

And Ivana, thinking about that nodded, "Yes."

Well, now, according to the data already noted, Ivana would have been about twenty-three when she went to Canada—Montreal specifically. If she was in Czechoslovakia—Gottwaldov—for fifteen years, that didn't figure at all.

The details were definitely unclear. They seemed to change from one version of her story to another. But one could always counter any suspicion of an evasion of the truth with the realization that life in Czechoslovakia during Ivana's formative years was not all sweetness and light. In fact, during her—presumably—last five years there (roughly 1968 to 1973) the Soviets were involved in military action in an effort to quell an uprising among the Czech people—smaller, but almost as fierce as the 1989 uprising that dumped the Communist government completely and brought a new look to Czech politics.

After the 1968 uprising was put down, the Czechoslovakian citizenry was not anywhere near as mobile as before—in point of fact, very few people were even allowed out of the country. The question arose whenever anyone speculated about Ivana: how, indeed, was Ivana able to emigrate?

The matter was still something to speculate about until February 1990, during the media uproar caused by the marital problems of Ivana and Donald Trump. The story that brought to light the manner in which Ivana outwitted the Czech authorities responsible for keeping Czechs within the Iron Curtain was originally broken in London by the *Sun*, a tabloid that specializes in the life styles of the rich and famous.

When the story broke, Ivana's lawyer, Michael Kennedy, immediately called a press conference in New York and revealed the truth. Whatever embellishments Ivana's team put on the original story were their own business, of course.

To understand the emigration ploy it is necessary to rethink the situation in Europe just after World War II. The countryside was in shambles. Most of the people could see only ruination and destruction all about them. Few of the economies were in any semblance of order. Hatreds engendered during the war years festered and threatened to break out anew as vengeance struggled against self-control.

America was untouched. America was the land of opportunity. To get to America—that was the goal of millions of destitute Europeans. By a provision of law, an American in Europe could marry a European and as the wife or husband of an American citizen, she or he would be welcome in America.

Thousands of people suddenly found themselves in love with American service personnel, married to them, and making the trek to freedom with perfect safety.

It was this knowledge that must have stimulated George Syrovatka's imagination. For, quite soon before he defected from Czechoslovakia, he apparently searched among his companions for a likely candidate to help Ivana out of the country. He knew no Americans in Czechoslovakia. But he did know Austrians, with whom he skied frequently.

George knew from experience, since he had defected from Czechoslovakia through Austria to the West, that an Austrian citizen could emigrate more easily than a Czech. Alfred Winklmayr was an Austrian citizen, probably a Viennese; Ivana did mention Vienna without prompting in her chat with Regis and Kathie Lee.

Winklmayr was, according to the press release, provided by Michael Kennedy, a skiing friend of Ivana and George's. "She didn't want to defect," Kennedy pointed out. "She could have defected, but that would have precluded her from seeing her parents."

And so Alfred and Ivana were married in November 1971 when Ivana was twenty-two and Alfred Winklmayr twenty-five, just about George's age.

Ivana's press conference, incidentally, corrected some errors of fact in the London *Sun* story, which had Herr Winkelmayr (note the different spelling) a "rich industrialist thirty-seven years [Ivana's] senior," who died within two years of the marriage, leaving Ivana enough money to finance her new life in Canada.

The truth was that Ivana simply married Alfred Winklmayr, used his—now her—Austrian citizenship to procure a passport, and left for Montreal, Canada, where George was waiting for her.

No fee was paid Winklmayr, Kennedy said. "He is a gentleman and did a very noble thing." It was a "Cold War marriage" that "was never consummated." In order to make that point very clear, Kennedy explained: "They never slept together."

The marriage was dissolved on August 2, 1973, in Los Angeles Superior Court.

An interesting contradiction, however, surfaced in a *Los Angeles Times* mention of the Winklmayr story picked up from the London *Daily Mail*. In the story, it was revealed that Winklmayr was now a real-estate salesman near Sydney, Australia, and happily married to his second wife. In the story, he disclosed that he had been asked to marry Ivana Zelnickova while he was working as a ski instructor in the United States.

In retrospect, the successful Cold War marriage ploy appears so neat and clean that it is amazing no one ever reconstructed it accurately. Except, of course, that all of the facts about Ivana's past were so shrouded in the mists of speculation that no one really cared to delve into them at any great depth for fear of drowning in them.

Now, of course, Ivana's hopscotching remarks to Regis Philbin and Kathie Lee Gifford can be seen as an allusion to how she was really able, with George's help, to work her way out of the web of political intrigue that bound up Czechoslovakia in the years after the Prague Spring turned into the Czechoslovakian winter of discontent.

And so, to recap, we do know that Ivana was born in Gottwaldov in 1949, that she was a ski racer of high quality, and that she came to Canada—to Montreal, actually—about 1972 or 1973. And we know that she got there through the help of George Syrovatka and Alfred Winklmayr, an Austrian who was probably a friend of both of them, in an arranged marriage to help out two of his friends.

With her Austrian passport, and Winklmayr's name on it, Ivana was not only able to leave Europe, but to come back to visit her parents in Czechoslovakia whenever she wanted.

We also know now that Winklmayr was not Ivana's mother's maiden name, as some researchers had speculated, but the name that Ivana took at the time of her marriage to her Austrian skiing friend. The mystery of Ivana's dual Canadian-Austrian citizenship mentioned in *People* magazine was also solved.

From there on the details of Ivana's comings and goings become a little bit clearer—although not enormously and conclusively so.

We pick up the story as Ivana arrives in Montreal, Canada.

Chapter Three
Stopover: Montreal

Like most young women in Europe, Ivana Zelnickova was multilingual. She knew Czechoslovakian, German, and French. In all three languages she was proficient enough to get along quite well wherever she was. Even if she had never known George Syrovatka, she might very likely have selected Montreal as a place to visit, if not to emigrate to. To many Middle Europeans this Canadian city was known as the gateway to the Promised Land—that is, the free Western world.

Located in eastern Canada in the province of Quebec, Montreal is the largest city in the Western Hemisphere whose first language is French. In fact, Montreal is second only to Paris as the largest, primarily French-speaking city in the world.

Ivana once said that she went to Montreal because she had an uncle there, with whom she wished to establish family relations. The term uncle can be interpreted in a number of ways, and even if there was no specific uncle related to her by blood ties, there certainly was a particular family with whom she wished to reestablish relations.

"Ivana had one family in Montreal that she knew very well from Czechoslovakia," is the way one of Ivana's associates expressed it. "She had come originally to Canada to visit relatives in Toronto." Indeed, in Toronto Ivana did have an aunt, by blood relationship, whom she visited several times.

But, of course, the Czechoslovakian family she knew very well was the Syrovatka family.

Ignoring all these details for the moment, it was obviously Montreal's cosmopolitan atmosphere that most intrigued Ivana and played an important role in persuading her to stay there once she made the break with Czechoslovakia—George or no George.

What also made Montreal different from other cities was the fact that it has a large English-speaking minority. There were actually so many minorities that the majority of the population belonged to some sort of minority. And it is an urban center, with, at that time, a million people living in the city limits, and another million in the suburbs.

It has long been considered the perfect stepping-stone between the Old World and the New World. Many who come to the Western Hemisphere with dreams of winding up in, say, New York or California, settle briefly in Montreal as they acclimate themselves to their new life style.

As for Ivana, she knew she could get along easily with her rapidly improving French, and she could even begin learning to live with the predominantly English-oriented people of North America.

Montreal is in no way behind the times. It is a waterfront city, located at the entrance of the Saint Lawrence Seaway, and thus serves as a nexus for North American people and a drifting population of individuals involved in transportation, communication, and commerce.

It has an historic Old City—Vieux Montreal—built right along the waterfront of the Saint Lawrence. It has a modern subway system that was opened in 1966. Montreal, in fact, pioneered the twentieth-century "belowground" life style of marketing, being the first metropolis to plan, construct, and maintain a genuine underground urban complex. It even beat out Toronto, timewise, in this extremely modern concept of shopping and living.

But to be quite frank about it, Ivana's move to Montreal has a much more practical orientation to it. George Syrovatka was there. And George had arranged her emigration from Czechoslovakia. He had settled down in an efficient three-room apartment on the eleventh floor of a residential building in Westmount, one of the better sections of Montreal.

He had opened a small ski boutique and sporting goods shop called "Top Sports." He also taught skiing, and spent a great deal of his working hours on the ski slopes of the Laurentian Mountains nearby and in the Vermont ski-resort areas.

Life was pleasant for Ivana in the centrally-located apartment, where she could see a panoramic view of the city. She also loved to putter around the apartment, buying new things to decorate the rooms.

One of the severest critics of her taste was Michael Syrovatka, George's kid brother. "She didn't really have a taste of her own," he said. "She would just get whatever she saw in the latest magazine. Then she would see something else in another magazine that wouldn't go with it, but she would get both those things just because each was the 'in' thing to get."

It was an easy life to settle into. From the beginning, Ivana loved the Montreal life style. Whether she ever admitted it to herself or not, she probably did want to get to New York sometime—if only to see and feel it. She was a top competitor—how could she even admit she did not want to see, to visit, to experience the best? New York was where everything important happened. It was the mecca for any Central European.

And as a mecca, it was harder to get to than Canada. Canada was open to traveling Europeans, and Montreal, with its large enclave of minorities, was the perfect port of entry for someone like Ivana. There she could become comfortable with the Western way of life that was so unlike that of her native Czechoslovakia with its strict Marxist code of ethics.

"Montreal," Ivana would say later, "was comfortable. Because it was so international, it was easy to settle there." Easy? No matter how you looked at it, for a woman—an only child—to leave her home in Czechoslovakia to seek a new life in the West was definitely a chancy thing, even with the support of a strong, self-sufficient man like George Syrovatka. But Ivana had been brought up by a good teacher, Milos Zelnicek, another self-sufficient man who taught her how to be self-reliant.

And so she took the chance. She was confident that George would help her up if she fell flat on her face.

Ivana was restless and anxious to get some kind of employment. Her skiing background was useful, but making money skiing was a highly competitive risk, and teaching skiing was totally impractical except as a part-time moonlighting venture. What Ivana needed was a career. Motion pictures? Modeling?

It was George who came up with a possible course of action for Ivana to pursue. A good-looking, successful, dynamic man himself, George was very much in demand by good-looking, successful, dynamic women. Many of these women held jobs as professional models. Others were designers. Still others were commercial artists. It was in this wide area that there should be some work for Ivana.

According to Yolande Cardinal, a producer of fashion shows in Montreal and head of Yocar Inc. (an acronym composed of her name), it was George who channeled Ivana into the business of show modeling in Montreal. "He had good contacts in the business," she said.

The way it turned out, George did not have to pick up Ivana when she fell flat on her face. She began making the rounds of the modeling houses in Montreal, seeking work, and she was quite readily snapped up and signed by one of the top modeling agencies in the Montreal area. It was owned and managed by Audrey Morris, who now owns and runs Audrey Morris Cosmetics in Fort Lauderdale, Florida.

Morris was impressed by Ivana from the day she met her. "A Czech designer I knew in Montreal called and told me she had a lovely girl she wanted me to meet. From there, it was just up all the way for Ivana. She was a natural for modeling. Very agile, she moved beautifully; she got that poise from her sports background."

Morris noted that Ivana was always very careful to project just the right image in every move she made. Her image had become an important facet of her overall character. Perhaps, Morris thought, her obsession with appearance came from her sporting background, where exercise and practice were always the highest priority. Looking right on the slopes had as much to do with being considered a successful skier as landing rightside-up at the bottom of a jump.

"Her grooming was always impeccable," Morris recalled. "There was never a hair out of place, and her nails were always polished. She did like a lot of heavy makeup, although that's more subdued now than it was then. But that was Ivana. Everyone recognized her as soon as she came out on the stage."

Morris was not alone in her appreciation of Ivana's talent for modeling. "I wish ten more like her would walk in the door right now," Kevin Johnson, the director of the Audrey Morris Agency, said recently. "She was just right. She was the perfect height and size and she had a good head for fashion."

Ivana, in her take-charge manner, assumed the responsibility for the development of her image. Exercise and sports took care of her figure; now she exerted control over her facial features. For example, her hair was tinted blonde. And she added a great deal of eye liner and lipstick to her makeup regimen.

Michael Syrovatka, for one, was not impressed with the

change. "I think she was prettier when she was in Czechoslovakia, when she still had dark hair—she has dark brown hair naturally—and a lot less makeup," he said. "The way she looked naturally was very pretty. But the blonde hair and all that makeup. . . ." He shrugged expressively.

Once Ivana had established her image, she stuck with it. And she was quite popular with the buyers and the women with whom she worked.

"She worked five years very closely with me," Cardinal said, "and that's how I got to know her. I hired her just after she had arrived here three months earlier." Cardinal was under the impression that Ivana was not really set on staying there or of even going to the United States.

But of course Ivana had George Syrovatka—and that, to Cardinal, was enough. "He was *gorgeous*," she said, "and a very nice guy. They were of the same age and they had the same language. They liked the same activities. They were both skiers, they were both swimmers, they both played tennis. That's all quite important. They were very much in love, and he supported and encouraged her modeling career."

Ivana more than held her own in her new profession. "She was a natural beauty, and very, very professional, very quiet, very well organized," Cardinal said. "You don't find that much with models. When you told her to be at a certain place at a certain time, she was there. She was very on time."

Ivana had learned the importance of timing in her sports training, and that sense of precise timing never deserted her. She was always conscious of the time, of the place, and of the program she was involved in. She was always *on*—to use a theatrical expression.

Cardinal said "She worked with veterans who had been in the business for a very long time and they knew what to expect from a good, professional model. She was hired by the best, best people in the business—companies, fashion coordinators."

"I worked with Ivana off and on for several years," Iona Monahan, fashion editor of the *Montreal Gazette*, said. Monahan was formerly employed by the *Montreal Star*, now defunct. "Montreal is not New York, and it's not Paris or London. Being a photographic model in those places is not the same thing as modeling in Canada, where you do little bits and pieces of everything."

And little bits and pieces of everything was exactly what Ivana was so very good at. And she never gave up trying to improve her modeling techniques. Persistence and her strong work ethic worked wonders, and helped her mold herself into the image the people who hired her wanted her to project.

"She would give everything she had in a show," Cardinal said, describing her onstage presence. "You knew that she would never make a mistake. She had a good memory, so she learned routines very well, and she had good contact with the other girls. Everyone respected her very much, and though I wouldn't say she had lots of models as friends, they all liked to work with her because they knew that onstage she would know her routine and wouldn't screw them up like some of the other girls."

Audrey Morris echoed Cardinal's impressions of Ivana's thorough professionalism. "Ivana worked hard at everything she did. Consequently, I was never leery of sending her out on a job. I always knew she would perform."

Nevertheless, there was a major communication difficulty at first, with Ivana unfamiliar with and totally befuddled by the English language. Morris came up with a solution that seemed to work. She would write out instructions to give to cab drivers to get Ivana where she was supposed to go, and she would give Ivana prompting in words to say to others, and so on.

Morris found Ivana an apt pupil and a quick study. It was largely through Morris's help that Ivana began to pick up the language and to sort it out in her mind so she could begin to think in English.

Both Morris and Cardinal sized up Ivana as a private and isolated person. "She did not pal around with the other models," Morris pointed out. That was not to say that she was unfriendly with anyone. "She was friendly, but she kept to herself. She was more into doing her work and then going home at the end of the day."

One thing that helped ineffably in her career was that George Syrovatka completely supported her modeling. "I'm glad she's found a job she enjoys," he told a newspaper writer. "She's in the age for modeling now. Maybe later on she can go into teaching." Even George was aware that modeling was not a lifelong career. And perhaps, too, he knew Ivana was meant for better things than parading her fashion expertise around on a stage.

Her hard work paid off rather quickly.

"The public and the buyers loved her," said Cardinal, "because of her charm and her professionalism. She was an instant hit. She was running from one place to the other all the time."

Her professionalism and her talent began to assert itself in a very positive way. And, at the same time, she found herself beginning to make good money.

"At that time, more than thirteen years ago, she was making up to fifty thousand a year," according to Cardinal. "That was a *lot of money* at the time in Montreal. She was one of the best. There were only two or three models in Montreal who were making that kind of money."

She bought herself her first car—a little red sports car. George had a BMW. They were both definitely upwardly mobile successes.

Of course, there were tiny flaws in her image—limitations of a very definite nature. No one is perfect. Morris pointed out, "Ivana was never considered a highly photogenic model. Her smile was too broad and sometimes she showed her gums." And that was apparently a no-no in the trade.

"Her pictures never succeeded in reflecting her true beauty," Morris said. That was the reason she did so much runway work, at which she excelled. There was rarely a fashion show without Ivana in it."

"The *Montreal Star* photographers worked with her a couple of times," Iona Monahan recalled. "But ninety-five percent of the work here at the time was fashion shows and showroom work." And there Ivana shone. "There were no major fashion publications. She was well-known within modeling circles. She worked for the best people here—stores like Holt Renfrew and Auckie Sanft, who is a top manufacturer, sort of like Bill Blass."

Soon Ivana was a fixture at Sanft's. She was not Sanft's numera una, but she was good enough to grace his showroom for some months, if not years.

"She did everything—all kinds of modeling—with the exception of haute couture," Morris said. Haute couture—or high fashion—was another of the small problems Ivana had. It was a specialty in itself, and the sine qua non for haute couture is a svelte kind of slinky tallness. A good haute couture model must be at least five feet nine or five ten. Ivana did not quite make it: at five foot seven and a half inches, she was too short!

There was life after modeling, however. Yolande Cardinal became a personal friend of Ivana's not because of her closeness to Ivana on the fashion-show runways, but because she and her husband were both good skiers who loved the slopes.

"I'm a sports fan, as Ivana is. We both went to exercise classes." The two couples—Cardinal and her husband and Ivana and George—would go skiing together on the weekends.

"We'd go to the Laurentians and a lot also to Stowe and Jay Peak in Vermont."

Jay Peak is located about an hour and a half from Montreal. Ivana and George made that trip regularly during the season. George had become a ski coach there, and Ivana soon got a job instructing the young people who wanted to make the ski team.

"It was the mountain-racing program for local kids, sort of like Little League," explained Mickey Doheney, a school director at Jay Peak, who knew Ivana and George. "They would pick up the kids at nine and go to the slopes probably until about three-thirty in the afternoon."

Doheney remembered Ivana, particularly, not only for the skills she had, but also for the difficulty she had in communicating with the kids.

"Ivana was a very smooth, good skier," he said, "although a lot of times the language barrier was a problem with the youngsters."

He remembered Ivana as being quite involved with her boyfriend at the time—George Syrovatka. He said that the two of them did not really associate much with the others on the slopes.

"We didn't hang around together that much. After work, some of us would go down to one of the bars on the mountain and have a beer or two. But Ivana and George weren't really a part of the drinking crowd. There was a definite drinking crowd; Ivana and George seemed a little more reserved."

Nevertheless, it was a tight community, so the skiing people go to know one another fairly well. There were about sixty or seventy instructors altogether. And, because the director at the time was a Czechoslovakian, "there was a pretty good Czech contingent. There were also a lot of Europeans on the staff at the time. It was an international type of ski school."

Doheney remembered that Ivana was a very pretty blonde, and he said that nobody ever made a move on her with George around. And George was always around. "He was a pretty big guy," Doheney said, "and she hung around with him very closely."

Doheney said that as far as he knew, Ivana had definitely been on the Czech national ski team, but whether or not she was in the Olympic Games in Sapporo, he did not know for sure. "I don't recall that being a highlight of her background."

George showed off his prowess at Jay Peak as a speed skier. He raced mostly in speed trial events, which were straight down-hills—Doheney explained: "No turns except the one where you try to stop at the bottom. You try to go as fast as you possibly can; the world record now is about 128 miles an hour. George at one point was the fastest North American skier; I think he did that in Cervinia, Italy, way back then."

Doheney remembered that Ivana and George were together for about two or three years. "I think she and George broke up after that," he said. "And George showed up with another gal whom he later married."

But then, that was all in the future.

Ivana was once asked why she bothered to teach children how to ski. She answered that she preferred to coach children rather than adults "because they are flexible. They copy you, and you can see results fast."

She explained in more detail. "Once, I had cut my finger and it was bandaged so I was holding my pole with this finger straight out. The second day I noticed all the kids had this finger straight out!" It was a good lesson to her.

"Other people can be too spoilt and everything goes slowly. The older ones want to do things they can't really manage. Then the ladies begin screaming because it's cold. No, I prefer to take the children."

Skiing on weekends in the Laurentians and at Jay Peak, work-ing during the week on the runways of Montreal's top fashion houses, spending her personal time with George Syrovatka—it was a wonderful life for Ivana Zelnickova.

And yet . . .

Ivana's parents made occasional visits to see her in Montreal. According to Yolande Cardinal, Ivana's father, Milos Zelnicek, was a "fantastic skier." For years, she recalled, he was a ski racing judge in international competitions. "He's very tall, athletic, and good-looking. Ivana was especially close to him. They're both

Olympic fans, and they would go to all the Olympics they could together."

Morris's description of Ivana's father matches Cardinal's. "Her father was very handsome, very tall and distinguished-looking, well-dressed, in good shape. He came over once or twice a year to visit Ivana. She was also so excited when he was coming into town, and he always came to see her fashion shows."

Ivana's mother, according to Cardinal, was apparently Austrian. "She's more of a mother—making sure that Ivana is well looked after, and looking after the kids. She took English so she could speak better." And, according to Morris, "Her mother was nice, friendly, somewhat on the rounder side, short. There was quite a difference between the two of them. Ivana has the svelte figure that her father had."

They would make a trip at least once a year, but only one would come at a time. "Her father would come one year and her mother another," Michael Syrovatka said. "I figured it was the only feasible way to do it because the trip did cost a lot of money."

They would spend time not only with Ivana and George, but with George's parents as well.

"What I remember about her mother was that she was short and plump." He did not remember whether or not Ivana's father had been a swimming champion, but he remembered him quite clearly.

The impression given by the visiting parents was that, although they were basically middle-class people, they seemed fairly well-off at the time—at least with enough money to make the pilgrimage to Montreal each year to pay tribute to Ivana.

For Ivana was certainly as much of a success as either of her parents could have imagined she might be. Little did they dream of what lay in the future for Ivana!

January and February are traditionally slow months in the modeling business. During that period, Ivana and George would travel to Europe to go skiing. There were several ski races in which George still participated. During their stay in Europe, Ivana would visit Gottwaldov to see her father and mother.

In the summer of 1975, Ivana and George flew to Cervinia, Italy, where George took part in the skiing meet that was being held there. In Cervinia every July there was a death-defying speed race on a twelve-thousand-foot-high glacier. Called the Flying Kilometer, this run was one of the hairiest and scariest in the world. Two years before, in 1973, George had set a new world record there, doing the downhill at 110.6 miles per hour.

Top speeds usually attained in downhill races were about eighty miles per hour, but the turns at the Flying Kilometer at Cervinia made it as suicidal as speed skiing, in which the world record was 120 miles per hour.

Life was next to perfect for Ivana. She had her relationship with George; she had her career in modeling; she had her mini-career in skiing; and she had an apartment to take care of. In addition, George had begun experimenting with a piece of ski equipment he had invented and was developing for cross-country skiing.

"He did very well with that," Cardinal once said. She described it as some variant of the traditional ski pole.

Although Ivana's parents treated the Syrovatkas as if they were family, and the Syrovatkas treated the Zelnicekovs as family, nothing formal was ever settled upon. Both Ivana and George had their own endeavors, in which each was incredibly active and successful. Their time together was simply a paralleling of two separate tracks, as it were. They were singles playing the couples game.

"I always considered George and Ivana as married," Michael Syrovatka once said. "In my family, marriage is just a formality. My parents treated Ivana as if she was their daughter-in-law. That's how George saw it, too."

In fact, Ivana was becoming interested in warming up the nest just a bit. She became excited about decorating George's apartment. And because she felt that she was doing well with her decorating, she began widening her horizons.

"My father had a weekend house in Brome Lake, about fifty miles outside Montreal," Michael Syrovatka said, "and Ivana would often go there with the family. She felt so at home there that she started to decorate the country house also! But there were some problems with that. Once I remember she put up some fake bricks on the wall just for the effect."

And how did George's parents react?

"As soon as she left, the bricks came off!" said Michael.

Ivana's fame—if her professionalism and her close attention to detail in her career could be called fame—became obvious to a larger world in late 1975 when a story appeared in print about Ivana and George. It actually featured Ivana, even though it was about the two of them. Titled "The Two Faces of Ivana—Model and Sportswoman," the story was published in the now-defunct *Montreal Gazette.*

In it, the writer, Margaret Haddrick, discussed this dual image of Ivana. Ivana told the writer she was strictly a self-made woman. "I never had a lesson or a modeling course, but I watched and copied the other girls. I was good in motion because of my sports training."

The writer suggested that at some point in the future, Ivana might well exchange the fashion showroom and runway for a teaching post in a high school or at a university. Not until the bookings dried up, Ivana pointed out.

Indeed, Ivana was quoted as being somewhat less than happy about modeling as a complete career. "If modeling becomes a career," she said, "there's no time to go to the theater, read books, and go on vacation."

Nor was ski racing a career goal, either. "I don't want to go to Europe, run all over the world to be first in some race!"

Ivana was perfectly candid with the newspaper writer, pointing out that she met George Syrovatka in Czechoslovakia when she was a teenager and he was a few years older than she. "They've been together ever since," the writer said.

Ivana was quoted as follows: "Modeling is a job to me, not a career. I have my social life, my husband, and my home."

Husband? Home?

This intriguing quotation once sent a New York researcher out after information about this hitherto unknown status. George Syrovatka was asked directly if he had been married to Ivana, and his response was an equivocal "not exactly."

Much more recently he was asked the same question. Now involved in real estate in Montreal, George Syrovatka said that he had definitely been a ski racer at the time he was with Ivana.

"She was a ski racer as well. We did not participate in the same races because they were different for men and for women, but on many occasions, the places and timing were the same. So we went together."

In answer to the question about their relationship, he replied, "I was never married to Ivana. There's no question about it."

He refused to be interviewed any further.

The appearance of the story in the *Montreal Gazette* was proof positive that Ivana had arrived—at least as a mini-celebrity. The fact that she was becoming someone important enough to write newspaper copy about may have given the Olympic Games Committee the idea to approach her about working for them.

Whatever the reason, Ivana was asked to help promote the 1976 Olympic Games to be held in Montreal. She agreed to do so with a group of Montreal models who were sent down to New York City to appear in some fashion shows and at the same time spread the good word about the summer Olympics in 1976.

And so in the summer of 1976, Ivana and two other models arrived in New York, did shows at Bonwit Teller's for Grosvenor Furs, and then spent some time on the town. One night the three of them went to Maxwell's Plum, a fashionable nightclub at its peak in the 1970s, but today just a memory. The place was packed, as it always was, but the three models waited patiently in line. Finally, the maitre d' came over and escorted them to a special table.

As he helped them into their seats, he pointed to a good-looking young man in the corner, and said: "Thanks to that guy."

Ivana bowed and waved to the man, saying, "Thank you very much," in her fractured English.

"Who is he?" Ivana later whispered to her companions, but none of them seemed to know.

When they left the nightclub, the maitre d' satisfied Ivana's curiosity. "That's Donald Trump."

Ivana smiled but shrugged. In Montreal, indeed in New York, the name Donald Trump was at that time the furthest thing from a household word. Ivana thought him a very decent sort who had simply helped them out with their seating arrangements during a crowded evening. Beyond that, she had no interest in him.

Cardinal, who knew nothing about this incident until some time later, went on with the story of their meeting.

"Donald never introduced himself that night," she said, "but he learned where the girls were staying in New York. He sent flowers over to Ivana the next day. That's how it started."

In fact, Ivana and Donald Trump did not even meet face-to-face on that trip. She was surprised when he called her on the telephone the next day. They talked several times, actually.

Then, a few weeks later, he traveled to Montreal to see a show Ivana was appearing in. This was a luncheon fashion affair at the Ritz Carlton.

"He just came to say hello to Ivana, and then he left," Cardinal continued.

Ivana was flabbergasted. She wondered, "My God! Why does he do this?"

Who was this man, Donald Trump? Ivana wondered.

Chapter Four
Middle America

Although the star of Donald J. Trump was indeed on the rise in 1976, it had not yet reached any appreciable apogee in the business firmament until a few years later as the seventies were winding down. That is not to say that people in the real-estate business were unaware of him. But the public itself was not fully cognizant of the dynamism of this young developer/builder/promoter/entrepreneur—the man who would eventually make his name as big and perhaps bigger than William Zeckendorf's in the world of Manhattan real estate.

His name had not yet penetrated the curtain of obscurity that veils most minor movers and shakers in the business community from the majority of the population before they become major contenders. Not yet was the name Trump known to people like Ivana and her two model friends, although they profited from his largess and personal interest at Maxwell's Plum. It would not be long before Trump would be as familiar a name to the average American as McDonald's or even Roy Rogers. But not yet.

Donald John Trump was born in August 1946, some three years before Ivana was born, in circumstances far removed and different from those that surrounded her birth. It was in environmental details that their initial appearances on earth differed, not in the essential makeup of their genes. It is a cliché to say that those who will be favored by celebrity later in life are usually marked from their beginnings, probably by high degrees of energy, vigor, and ambition—characteristics most likely inherited from their forebears.

It was true certainly of Donald Trump.

The newborn was a mixture of Swedish and Scottish stock. Donald's father, Frederick Charles Trump, was born in New Jersey on October 11, 1905, the son of a roustabout restaurant owner who died when his son was only eleven years old. Fred's seamstress mother brought him up single-handedly, and he became first a carpenter, then an architect and engineer, studying at the

Pratt Institute in Brooklyn, New York. But his basic talent was always entrepreneurship. When he was only eighteen years old, he formed a company in 1923 to build houses in Woodhaven, Queens, New York.

In 1935 Fred Trump married Mary MacLoed, an immigrant from Scotland. Donald was their fourth child; after Maryanne, born in 1937; Fred, Jr., born in 1938; and Elizabeth in 1942, when World War II was still in full swing. There would be one more son, Robert, born in August 1948.

Construction work stalled during the years of the Great Depression, but Fred Trump was able to utilize money from the Federal Housing Authority to put up residential structures for the homeless during those tough years.

Once the war was over, building boomed—and Fred Trump's fortunes zoomed dramatically upward. It was under the most auspicious of circumstances that Donald J. Trump was born—in a twenty-three-room house in Jamaica Estates in Queens, New York; the house in an exclusive section that his father had built.

The young Trumps, like the Kennedy's, were brought up in an atmosphere of competition and ambitious endeavor not ordinarily present in homes of such obvious affluence.

"Life's a competition," Fred Trump told a magazine writer. "I brought my kids up in a competitive environment."

Competition in the Trump household was different than the competition in the household of Ivana Zelnickova. It was a competition of the mind, of the spirit, of the psyche; not of the muscles, of the reflexes, of the trained body. Yet, it had an influence on the Trump offspring not unsimilar to the influence that sports competition exerted on the attitude and mind-set of Ivana.

Of five children, four rose to positions of prestige and eminence.

Donald Trump's sister Maryanne Trump (later Barry) eventually became a federal judge in Trenton, New Jersey.

Donald's sister Elizabeth became an administrative assistant with the Chase Manhattan Bank.

Donald Trump had spectacular successes in real estate and construction.

Donald's younger brother, Robert, turned out to be Donald's closest associate and right-hand man in the enormous Trump Organization.

It was Fred, Jr., who did not quite fit the mold. Although he tried to conform to the rigorous tradition of overachievement that was the norm in the Trump family, for some reason he did not seem able to toe the mark, and in 1981 he died, largely of health complications resulting from alcoholism.

Young Donald grew up in love with the excitement of his father's work. He would go with him to visit building sites, and, later, he would spend summers working on Trump construction projects or helping out in the Trump rent-collection offices. Only a winter vacation, usually in Florida, and a week in the summer, at Grossinger's in the Catskills, broke up the monotony of the Trump life style—dedicated, as it were, strictly to the business of building and maintaining income-producing properties.

Even in their religion the Trumps were not ordinary New Yorkers. They were members of the congregation of the Marble Collegiate Church on Fifth Avenue in New York. The minister there had made a great name for himself by producing a best-selling book that gave him instant fame in the early 1950s. It was called *The Power of Positive Thinking*; the minister's name was Dr. Norman Vincent Peale.

Donald and his siblings were educated at Kew Forest School, a private educational institution on the edge of Forest Hills, which was even more posh a community than Jamaica Estates. But it was Donald who, from the beginning, exhibited all the manifestations of hyperactivity and overachievement, especially at school.

Everything he did he did with élan, trying to outdo everyone else in an orgy of competitive furor. Even walking down the street, Donald would run to keep ahead of everyone else. It was impossible for him to remain in the center of a group; he always had to be ahead where he could outstrip others.

In school he was an incorrigible, impossible little hellion. He would throw cakes around at birthday parties, toss erasers at teachers, and squirt soda pop at the girls on the playground at lunchtime. No one seemed able to curb his talent for mischief. Even his father could not keep him in line. A frown from Fred, Sr. would suffice for Robert or Fred, Jr., but it simply brought on further rebellious outbursts from Donald.

"I used to fight back all the time," Donald told a writer at *New*

York magazine. "My father was one tough son-of-a-gun. My father respects me because I stood up to him."

Whether the latter statement is true or not, the fact was that even Fred, Sr. could not put down the irrepressible, hyperkinetic Donald. But school officials at Kew Forest School were insistent that something be done about him. Things dragged on with Fred, Sr. promising to bring his son into line, but with no evidence of it at school.

Finally, in 1959, Fred Trump got fed up with Donald's antics, and transferred him to the New York Military Academy, a prep school for children of the affluent. It was located in Cornwall-on-Hudson on the west bank of the Hudson River in Putnam County.

Donald's hyperactivity continued unabated even at "Neema," which was what the Academy was called. Donald got good grades when he put his mind to it, achieving the classification of Honor Cadet (an average of eighty-five percent or better). He liked his uniform and looked good in it. And in spite of his size and weight, which were about average, he was good at sports—particularly at baseball.

On the social level, it was a different story. Every week Neema would hold social affairs for the cadets, including dances and parties. Donald's status at Neema was not of a top level. He was obviously nouveau riche—an arriviste whose money was new and tainted with crass commerciality rather than old and pure. Because of his lack of social status, he was rather "out of it." But he was a big enough hit to be voted Neema's "Ladies Man" by his peers. And that was odd because women were not really Donald Trump's main interest in life at that time.

He graduated in 1964, an Honor Cadet for four of his five years, and was the recipient of the Coach's Award in baseball.

"He was a real leader," Colonel Theodore Dobias, his baseball coach, recalled. "He was even a good enough first baseman that the White Sox sent a scout to look at him."

But Donald's aim was to continue on through college before going to work for his father. He chose Fordham University in the Bronx.

During his first year at Fordham—in November 1964—Donald and his father attended the opening of the Verrazano-Narrows

Bridge linking Staten Island and Brooklyn. During these ceremonies something happened that was an eye-opener to him.

Dozens of dignitaries attended, among them Robert Moses, New York's Parks Commissioner; Nelson Rockefeller, governor of New York State; Sergio Fenoaltea, the Ambassador from Italy; Abe Stark, borough president of Brooklyn; Robert Wagner, mayor of New York City; Francis Cardinal Spellman of the Archdiocese New York. These officials all gave grandiose introductions to one another and then proceeded to compliment one another on their sagacity and genius in creating the marvelous span over the Narrows. It was obvious to Donald that in many instances men who had opposed the project from the beginning were now receiving hosannas for being responsible for the bridge's existence.

Interestingly enough, there was one man who was not introduced or mentioned by name: Othmar H. Ammann, the eighty-five-year-old engineer and bridge expert who had designed the bridge. And Donald Trump was one of the few people present who realized that Ammann was the man without whose genius the bridge never would have been built.

This omission was not lost on Donald J. Trump.

"I realized then and there, that if you let people treat you how they want, you'll be made a fool," Trump later told a newspaper reporter. "I realized then and there something I would never forget: I don't want to be made anybody's sucker."

Meanwhile, Donald's education was proceeding on another level. It was not long before Donald and Fordham University discovered that they were not made for one another. The mind-bending theosophy of the Jesuits and the intellectual gymnastics of the followers of St. Ignatius of Loyola soon convinced Donald that his future must lie elsewhere. The five years of spit-and-polish at Neema had been no summer vacation, but, compared to Jesuitical cant, it seemed almost like a relaxed and laid-back paradise.

He wanted out. But his father wanted him to finish his college education. About that he was adamant. Their confrontation continued for some months before a compromise was eventually hammered out.

Donald's aim was to quit school and go to work for his father. His father's aim was for Donald to get a college education and then come to work for him.

Donald wanted out right now. His father refused to let him quit immediately.

The compromise was a simple one. Donald agreed to get a college degree. His father agreed to take him on when he had the degree. Within those parameters, Donald could work out the details.

Thus, Donald decided to transfer from Fordham to another institution that would teach something closer to what he had in mind. What he wanted to study was business. Then he would be able to learn about selling the houses his father was building.

Donald decided on Wharton, one of the best business colleges in the country, located on the University of Pennsylvania campus in Philadelphia.

His grades were never a problem, and when he applied for transfer, he was accepted and made the move during his second year at Fordham. Once in Pennsylvania, he settled down to finish his college education so he could go to work for his father.

But Wharton was disappointing. The classroom routine bored him. He was more interested in real business deals that were being made outside the campus—deals having to do with real estate and construction. Theory, Donald decided, was for the birds. Donald wanted to be where the action was. Reading and thinking about something, he decided, was never as exciting as doing it.

As a result, he tended to be somewhat different from the average business college student. As at Neema, he was in the center of the classroom action, but not really part of it.

One of the most obvious differences about him was the fact that he did not drink or smoke. In the 1960s, anyone on a college campus who neither drank nor smoked was something of a kook. In fact, anyone who did not smoke pot or do drugs was considered out of it. In those days, the term was square.

Donald Trump was a square at Wharton.

It is well for the reader to realize that the country—in fact, the world—was undergoing one of its periodic revolutions in life-style. The word life style itself rose from that era. Only those under thirty years of age were considered actively alive. Smoking, drinking, drugging, carousing, doing your own thing, and the permissive life were all in.

But Donald was old before his time. His mind was on business when the minds of most of his peers were on pot, permissiveness, and hard rock music. Donald knew he was something of an alien—a stranger in a strange land.

But in defense Donald Trump adopted an attitude that might be termed cocky by some, arrogant by others, and downright rude or snobbish by still others. The fact that he was given to flashy clothes that were just slightly off did not help him to win friends or influence people either.

Like all true entrepreneurs, Donald Trump kept his eyes and ears open even while he was coasting through Wharton. One day he read in the papers that a twelve-hundred-unit apartment complex in Cincinnati, Ohio, was being foreclosed. Federally financed, Swifton Village had fallen onto hard times. There were eight hundred vacant apartments, and the development was floundering. The developers had gone under and the government had foreclosed on the village.

Donald studied the property firsthand and found that no one had put in a bid for it. He knew that in cases in which a government agency became involved in a foreclosure the bureaucracy sometimes simply wanted to get out from under the mess as quickly as possible. The agency was just not equipped to manage and maintain the property.

This was the case with Swifton Village. And in this situation, the government wanted out in the worst possible way.

Donald Trump discussed Swifton Village with his father. Fred, Sr. realized that his son was probably right. He agreed to follow Donald's lead and so the two of them, using Trump money, put in a very minimal bid. Two years earlier, the place had been built at a cost of twelve million dollars. The Trumps bid half of that—six million. The government immediately closed on the bid. Not only that, the Trumps were able to arrange a mortgage for the entire six million, plus about a hundred thousand, which they used to fix up the place.

Donald Trump had known without studying theory that to buy a project without putting any money at all down was the best of all possible real estate deals. And, of course, if the Trumps could get the place running well, they could cover their mortgage payments with the rent itself.

Swifton Village was a shambles. Some of the tenants had ripped their places apart. It was not easy to get rid of the bad tenants, but the Trumps managed it. Then the Trumps spruced up the place and made it not only livable, but attractive as well.

What they essentially did was perform an extensive cosmetic job on the building—installing new shutters, shaping up the brick surfaces, and so on.

By the time the interior was refurbished—the halls painted, the floors sanded and stained—the Trumps were running huge advertisements in the Cincinnati papers to promote the idea of a *new* Swifton Village.

And the advertising paid off. Within a year, it was one hundred percent rented.

Donald Trump did not want to be an apartment-complex manager. He wanted to get out and move on to new things. Within a few months, Donald had put Swifton Village up for sale and had an interested buyer.

Moreover, the Trumps sold the refurbished Swifton Village for twelve million dollars—exactly the same amount the original builders had paid to construct it.

The Trumps made a profit of about six million dollars on the deal. This was business as far as Donald was concerned—not reading books about it at Wharton.

In May 1968 Donald Trump graduated from Wharton School of Business with a B.S. degree in economics. He was anxious to get to work in his chosen field—real estate—now that he had got his feet wet in his Cincinnati project. What he really wanted to do was . . .

According to his autobiography, *Trump: The Art of the Deal*, Donald Trump was personally worth about $200,000 when he graduated—not bad for someone who had been in school most of his life. The money, however, was all tied up in real estate in Brooklyn and Queens. Trump was aware that real estate was very hot right then in Manhattan.

Frankly, Donald wanted to make it big not in Brooklyn or Queens, but in Manhattan. "I had my eye on Manhattan from the time I graduated," he wrote. But Fred Trump listened to his son Donald's persuasive spiels in silence. Then he would rush down to Florida, or over to New Jersey, or out to Nevada to look over some hot prospects but, to Donald's disappointment, never in Manhattan.

Donald Trump's first assault on New York City was to relocate physically in Manhattan. He took an apartment and became a New Yorker in the sense that he actually lived there.

Next, he initiated an active social life. Although he had never really been a ladies' man in college, he started to frequent all the posh haunts in New York City where upwardly mobile beauties were searching out rich, unmarried, and upwardly mobile males.

Still a nondrinker and nonsmoker—*still* not fashionable attributes—Donald Trump dated an extensive list of trendy and beautiful feminine models, actresses, and dancers.

When his father asked him if he was getting serious about anyone, Donald replied characteristically that he had met a lot of women, but "their heads are all screwed on wrong."

Le Club was *the* club in the late sixties. It was the hottest place going at the time. It was also exclusive and hard to get into. In fact, you had to be invited. And no one was about to invite Donald Trump. After all, he was new money. He was in real estate.

Donald Trump, however, had not lost the arrogance that had been part of his character through Neema, Fordham, and Wharton. He telephoned the manager of Le Club.

"I'd like to join your club," he said.

There was a burst of amused laughter on the other end of the line. And then there was silence. The connection was broken.

The next day Donald called again, demanding access to the president of the club. "I want to send him something."

No luck. Then Donald called the president of Le Club and told him that he wanted to join. This time there was a bit of conversation that proved to be amusing, if nothing else. Finally the president succumbed to Donald's persistence, and suggested:

"Why not meet me for a drink at Twenty-One?"

Donald met the president and a friend of his at Twenty-One. The two of them liked to drink; Donald did not drink. About ten o'clock that night, Donald related in his autobiography, he "practically had to carry them home."

A week or so later, Donald called the president once again. The president could not recall his name; apparently it had been lost in a drunken fog. There was, however, another date set up at Twenty-One. At that meeting, the president of Le Club finally agreed to put Donald up for membership.

"I was admitted to the Club," Donald wrote, "and it turned

out to be a great move for me, socially and professionally. I met a lot of beautiful young single women, and I went out almost every night." But it was no picnic. "These were beautiful women, but many of them couldn't carry on a normal conversation. Some were vain, some were crazy, some were wild."

Donald Trump went everywhere: Elaine's, Regine's, Twenty-One, Le Club; he knew he had to be seen. And he was seen. One woman remembers him as a "kind of fringe member of the social crowd." Still out of it. Almost in, but not really.

By the beginning of 1973, Trump properties in the New York area were valued at about $150 million, with out-of-town Trump holdings valued at maybe $50 million. The aggregate worth of the Trump Organization had grown from $40 million to $200 million during the five years Donald Trump had been working for his father. And that was a good solid five hundred percent increase!

And so Fred Trump finally deferred to the wishes of his son.

"I gave Donald free rein," Fred told the *New York Daily News*. "He has great vision, and everything he touches seems to turn to gold."

Free rein meant the goal that Donald Trump had always envisioned in the back of his mind: New York, New York!

But before New York could be tackled, a problem surfaced—a legal move made against the Trump empire itself. It involved a charge of racial discrimination against the Trump Organization, with the United States Justice Department accusing the Trumps of discriminatory renting practices against blacks.

The Trumps denied the charge as "absolutely ridiculous. We have never discriminated and we never would. There have been a number of local actions against us and we've won them all. We proved in court that we did not discriminate."

They pointed out that of the sixteen thousand units in question more than seven hundred were rented to blacks at the time. They then filed a hundred million dollar lawsuit against the federal government, charging that the Justice Department, in accusing the Trumps of racial discrimination in their renting policies, made "irresponsible and baseless charges against the realty company."

Later on, they said, "We never discriminated against blacks. Five to ten percent of our units are rented to blacks in the city. But we won't sign leases with welfare clients unless they have guaranteed income levels, because otherwise, everyone immediately starts leaving the building."

Roy Cohn, who became famous as one of the late Senator Joseph McCarthy's lawyers during the McCarthy hearings in 1954, was now representing Donald Trump.

"The Trumps performed so perfectly under the consent decree that expired last June that the government made no move to extend it," Cohn said. "Today's motion is nothing more than a rehash of complaints by a couple of planted malcontents, not one of which has the slightest merit."

The Justice Department agreed that the Trump Organization had, "in some instances, accomodated the needs of individual complainants. But it has not taken adequate action to prevent future violations."

The case was eventually settled out of court when Donald Trump signed an agreement providing open housing opportunities for minority groups.

The move into New York real estate became a reality in 1973 for Donald Trump. For a long time now, he had wanted a piece of property that lay along the Hudson River. As he drove along the West Side Highway, he would see it and think about it time and time again.

It was an abandoned railroad yard that stretched from Fifty-ninth Street all the way up to Seventy-second Street along the riverfront. He knew it belonged to the Penn Central Railroad.

In 1973 the Penn Central Railroad was in the midst of a bankruptcy filing. To carry out their proceedings, the railroad had hired a man named Victor Palmieri to sell off all the assets of the line. These assets included the abandoned yards in the West Sixties, as well as another yard located in the West Thirties, running from West Thirtieth Street to West Thirty-ninth Street between the Hudson River and Tenth Avenue at one end of Eleventh Avenue at the other. Contained therein were long stretches of abandoned buildings, rundown warehouses, and miles of track.

Penn Central's deal with Palmieri was that Palmieri would take a percentage of the sale every time he could find a buyer for any of the particular assets Penn Central owned.

The year 1973 was not a good year for New York City itself— let alone the Penn Central Railroad. The city was the closest it had ever been to bankruptcy. A combination of factors was causing the trouble.

First of all, the federal government had finally announced a moratorium on all housing subsidies. These subsidies had been the mainstay of construction in the city for years. Secondly, interest rates were beginning to rise, too, after remaining stable for many years. And at the same time the interest rates were going up, precluding businessmen from borrowing money to provide cash for construction, inflation had begun to plague the economy.

In addition to these three important factors, the city was beginning to dig itself into a deep hole of debt. Even the politicians were beginning to shake a bit over the amount of the debt. There was talk about bankruptcy for the city—and this rumor was fed by the press, which could always sense a good story even before it broke it.

Construction was on the skids. Within a year, the number of housing starts plummeted from fifteen thousand to six thousand.

Now, with all these important factors making it rough to build and to sell, Donald Trump knew that it was the optimum time to purchase property that was underpriced. And most property in the city was underpriced to a fantastic degree. And the most appallingly underpriced were those two abandoned railyards owned by the Penn Central.

And so, with his usual mixture of arrogance and self-assurance, Donald Trump telephoned Palmieri, introduced himself, and told him outright that he wanted to make a deal to purchase the Penn Central Railroad's Sixtieth Street railyards. Palmieri was at first amused and then interested—so much so that he invited Donald Trump in to talk to him.

By the time the two of them met and assessed each other— Trump described Palmieri later as "a very smooth, attractive guy, an Italian who looked like a WASP"—they were ready to cut a deal of some kind.

After the usual sparring and backing and filling, it was decided that not only the Sixtieth Street yards would be included in the sale, but the Thirtieth Street yards as well.

Palmieri had the real estate. And he had the go-ahead to sell it. Trump had connections with the just-elected mayor, Abe Beame (nurtured through his father's connections with Beame), and he could come up with the money as well.

There was only one problem. And it was an immense one.

Donald Trump had absolutely no track record at all in swinging deals of this kind, especially in New York, which was the toughest place of all to pull any deal off. He might be able to work it. At the same time, he might fail. The big problem he had was to convince Palmieri and his people that he could get the financing and pull off the sale.

Trump and Palmieri drew up agreements giving Trump the exclusive option to purchase the Sixtieth Street and Thirtieth Street yards, subject to zoning, subject to approval of the court handling the bankruptcy, and subject to various other details.

Donald Trump had a good idea of what he wanted to use the property for. What the city was in a crying need for at that time was affordable housing. Trump had a plan to build middle-income housing with rents at about $110 to $125 a room through financing from a government subsidy program.

But there were other uses to which he could put the land. Of course, the idea of affordable housing was a very attractive talking plan. It sounded good. Donald Trump knew it would appeal to the politicians who would have to okay it.

What Donald needed most of all was what he would be getting from Palmieri—credibility in the real-estate industry. And credibility with the public. New York City was in the doldrums. Something had to get it back on track.

"Those properties were nothing but a black hole of undefinable risk," Palmieri told a financial writer in explaining why he had chosen to sell them to Donald Trump. "We interviewed all kinds of people who were interested in them, none of whom had what seemed like the kind of drive, backing, and imagination that would be necessary. Until this young guy Trump came along. He's almost a throwback to the nineteenth century as a promoter. He's bigger than life."

And so on July 29, 1974, Donald Trump held a press conference and announced that the Trump Organization had secured options to buy the two abandoned railyards at $62 million. The story hit the front page of *The New York Times*.

What made the story worth that kind of play—a major spot in one of the most prestigious and widely read newspapers in the world—was the fact that Donald Trump had secured those options from Palmieri *without laying out one red cent of his own money!*

The next thing to do, of course, was to get the city interested enough to back low-cost housing on the sites.

Trump spent a great deal of time with the newly-elected mayor, Abe Beame, trying to talk him and his associates into backing his purchase and his idea to build housing on it.

Of course, that meant that Donald Trump had to go, hat in hand, to all the politicians on the City Planning Commission, the Board of Estimate, and many other local community boards to elaborate on his plans.

It was quite evident that most of these people, having just been elected to office or designated by elected politicians to these offices, were trying to sample the winds of public opinion so that they would know which direction to move in. It would be suicide for them to back someone who would not produce, or who might produce something that would not be acceptable to the general public.

They might well stall on making any decision on the subsidization of a development like the one Donald Trump envisioned. The time was not ripe for a project of this kind. One by one various disasters unfolded that showed the city to be in even worse shape than had been previously thought.

None of these developments helped Trump. If anything, most of them proved that Trump had been wrong in trying to make a move at this time.

In February 1975 the Urban Development Corporation, a state agency that peddled bonds to finance public housing, defaulted on a hundred million dollars in repayment. In September 1975 the mayor of New York announced that the city was suspending its own plans to finance the construction of almost all new housing. And in November 1975 the state of New York announced that it was suspending all financing of lower- and middle-income housing *for five years.*

As Donald Trump learned, the name Trump conveyed no magic to anyone at that point in his career. Yes, he had constructed housing projects in remote places, but not in Manhattan. Yes, he had purchased, refurbished, and sold housing projects for good gain. Yes, his father had a great track record for producing housing units.

But for the deal he was making here—to turn the two abandoned railyards into viable properties to house thousands of New Yorkers—Donald Trump had a track record that was, in the current phrase, zip. No wonder one of his close friends was told by an associate: "Trump has a great line of shit, but where are the bricks and mortar?"

Where, indeed, were the bricks and mortar?

In the mind of Donald Trump.

Could he work it out, or would he wind up back in Queens, helping his father collect rents?

No wonder, too, that when he met and was attracted to Ivana Zelnickova she had heard nothing about him. And yet, in spite of the fact that he had a lot on his mind—the success or failure of his entire career, actually—he decided to commit himself to her just as he had decided to commit himself to doing something big with those abandoned railyards that bordered the Hudson River.

Chapter Five
The Courtship of Donald Trump

Within a very short time of her original meeting with Donald Trump, Ivana Zelnickova realized that her life had suddenly arrived at one of those dramatic turning points. These seemed to be occurring at increasingly shorter intervals in her life.

She had already made an important choice several years before when she had decided to leave Czechoslovakia to emigrate to Canada.

But this new direction that now beckoned would certainly involve an even more fundamental change in her day-to-day existence, and would indeed entail an entirely new course from which she would not be able to turn back.

She sensed it from the beginning, even if she did not try to sit down and analyze it. Whether she struggled over her options is of course not known; Ivana was never one to discuss her inner problems with anyone except in a superficial way.

And yet occasionally her attempts at self-analysis surfaced in conversations with others—even about what attracted her to Donald Trump and what attracted him to her.

"I think what attracts us so much together is not only the love and all that stuff," Ivana said. "It's the energy. We are very much alike in that way. I can't sit still."

Ivana would be the first to admit that when she met Donald Trump, it was not love at first sight—no enchanted evening across a crowded room, or a brilliant flash of instantaneous enlightenment. "I wasn't an eighteen-year-old girl," she explained. "I didn't get excited immediately."

In fact, they were to date for the better part of a year just to get used to one another. And during that time Ivana became aware that Donald was very much like her. Although opposites generally attract, there must be an elemental bonding to make it work.

"Energy," she would say later. "That fabulous energy. You

see people who are doers, they have this energy, this life, this spark. It's part of Donald that that energy gets from one person to another. He's just a great leader, the way he motivates people." But that was all in the future.

Meanwhile, Ivana continued as best she could to adhere to her daily routine, to steep herself in the familiar while she dreamed of and vied with the unfamiliar. And yet the inner struggle she was having was, if not obvious, at least noted by those close to her.

Shortly after their first meeting at Maxwell's Plum, Ivana and Donald Trump began going out together. On their first real date, Donald came to Montreal. After that they began seeing one another mostly in New York, but sometimes elsewhere. Hardly ever, if the truth be told, in Montreal.

When the trips Ivana made to New York became more and more frequent, Audrey Morris knew there was a great deal going on behind the scenes with Ivana and Donald Trump.

"Ivana would go down to New York for some long weekends, and she would let us know so we'd be sure not to book her at that time," she said.

Yolande Cardinal remembered the first winter that followed Ivana and Donald's meeting in 1976. The story went that Ivana had mentioned in passing to Donald Trump that she was going with a group of her skiing friends to Aspen over the New Year's holiday.

"She had gone to Aspen each of the five years she lived in Montreal with a group of friends who, like her, had no family or relatives in Montreal," Cardinal said. "Donald heard about it and decided to go, too. The problem was that he did not know how to ski."

And, of course, he knew that he would not be making points with Ivana by not knowing how to do the thing that she loved to do the best. Donald Trump's solution to that problem was typical of the man. In addition, it was proof positive that his relationship with Ivana Zelnicekova was not a shallow and insignificant one.

What he did was this: Two weeks before Ivana and her group were to arrive in Aspen, he flew out to Colorado and took a crash course in skiing with a private tutor. He was no slouch as an athlete, of course. He had been good in both high school and in college, in spite of the fact that he was not hugely built.

In typical fashion, he was ruthless with himself, becoming familiar with every nuance of the sport, and prodding himself mercilessly until he was able to master the basic skills and even show some style in doing them.

After Ivana arrived with her friends, the two of them went out on the slopes the next morning. It was with pleasant surprise that Ivana found Donald Trump to be a fairly self-confident skier.

According to Cardinal, Ivana was much taken by this proof of Donald Trump's interest in her.

"She was very much impressed with both his skiing ability and with the fact that he had taken lessons to be able to go skiing with her," she said. "She is a very determined woman, and she definitely likes it when someone else shows determination of the kind she exhibits."

Ivana herself admitted that his learning to ski so rapidly gave her an insight into Donald Trump's competitiveness. "He's very competitive, and so am I," she said. She once jokingly referred to his skiing ability in this fashion: "When Donald finally saw me ski down the mountain, he took off his skis and said he would never put them on again." Then she chuckled, deep in the throat. "But of course, he did," she went on.

As for Donald Trump, he once mused: "Ivana is almost as competitive as I am."

That winter outing turned out to be a very important one for Ivana and Donald. It was in Aspen, as they sat around indulging in a bit of apres-ski talking and laughing, that Donald confided to Ivana that she seemed to be just the type of woman that he would like to marry.

Ivana took this information with the usual grain of salt, knowing that the things men said in romantic settings generally turned out to be overkill at best. But at the same time, she was impressed with the fact that he seemed honest, straight forward, and credible.

"She still didn't know that he had a really lot of money," Cardinal said. "He never told her anything about that. In the beginning, he was playing the role of an ordinary working Joe." With Ivana, that was the perfect role to play. After all, she was making good money; there was no reason for her to dig gold out of men. She just wanted to meet good people.

But talk of marriage sobered her. Just the hint that here was a man who was taken enough with her to mention marriage put a whole new dimension on her interest in him. Ivana had been brought up in a good, tightly structured family. All her instincts pointed toward a strong family life; with a husband, with children, with a solid relationship.

Yolande Cardinal could guess what was going on inside Ivana's mind. It was a confrontation, pure and simple. And the confrontation was between Ivana and George Syrovatka.

"She wanted to get married to George," Cardinal said, quite sure about her facts. (After all, she knew them both.) "She wanted children and a family."

Although Ivana did not talk about it to anyone else—probably not even to Yolande Cardinal—it was very much in her mind that her relationship with George had remained on a plateau for years and did not seem likely ever to change. In fact, it seemed as if her relationship with George was not heading anywhere at all.

What Cardinal could guess, and what Ivana's other confidants could guess, was that Ivana was now to a point where she was taking serious stock of herself. Here she was, going on to twenty-eight years of age, still unmarried. Yes, she was making good money. Yes, she was pursuing a career that she loved.

But there was always that other consideration, that consideration that every career-oriented women must feel. She would have been the first to admit that she wanted a husband, that she wanted kids, that she wanted to be a mother, that she wanted to head a family—that she wanted more out of life than being one of two singles playing at doubles.

When would she be able to settle down to have a family?

There was never any indication that she and George Syrovatka had ever sat down face-to-face and discussed marriage with one another. Yet, it is quite probable that they did. It was obvious, however, that George's point of view prevailed. He was not interested in marriage right at that moment. Maybe later.

But time was passing and Ivana was beginning to count the months and years. For some reason, she was not able to get George to see her point. She was getting older. She wanted kids. Why not settle down and have them?

And now—with another man actually saying the magic word marriage to her—Ivana knew that her tenuous relationship with George would never be the same again. Perhaps she told him the facts. Perhaps she did not. If he was forced to face the facts, he obviously did not change his mind one whit. At the end of whatever confrontation they had, the status quo remained unchanged. George was not yet ready to settle down and marry.

To Yolande Cardinal, the problem seemed to reside in George Syrovatka's nature, in his personality. She had known him for some time, and she thought she could read an immaturity in him.

"George was not mature enough or ready for marriage at all," Cardinal said. She felt that then had been a bad time to suggest making such a change in his life style. Cardinal had heard that there was some vague problem hovering over George at the time: some obscure details about his papers. After all, he had defected from Czechoslovakia. Perhaps there was still some unfinished business to be resolved regarding his citizenship.

Perhaps when George defected and settled in Montreal—after all, he had been forthright about that and had even mentioned it to the newspaper reporter who wrote the piece about Ivana and him—his citizenship had never really been straightened out.

Because of the still unsettled political situation in Czechoslovakia, at that time, such a problem might take months, years' even, to work out. And while that paperwork was being done, perhaps he was unable to make any commitment to marriage, especially with his own legal identity somewhere out there in limbo.

To look at the situation from George's point of view, he might well have considered it unfair to Ivana to become enmeshed in the web of bureaucratic contradictions and minutiae that it would take to straight his papers out. To her, of course, it appeared at the time that George was simply not interested in marriage. It was, in effect, the wrong time of his life to make such an important and complicated move.

It must be pointed out that this speculation about paperwork is strictly extrapolation based on guesswork, and not based on any hard facts whatsoever. Nevertheless, such an impediment to marriage may have definitely been there.

Audrey Morris, too, saw a change in Ivana once she had met Donald Trump, a change that was evident to almost anyone close to her. The change demonstrated that she did indeed have a problem.

"It was definitely a conflict for Ivana when she met Donald," she said. "George was a good skier, a good looker, very sportive, and highly intelligent." But, of course, it was obvious that he was not yet ready for marriage, for whatever the reason.

Ivana even went so far as to ask Morris for advice about how to handle the two men in her life—something she had never done before and something that was definitely out of character for her. To Morris this was significant. She knew that Ivana was very much concerned about her future and about her relationship with these two attractive men.

Morris also knew that the decision Ivana was forcing herself to make would hurt her terribly, and hurt someone she loved terribly, too.

"She chatted with me about it a few times," Morris said.

By now Ivana was beginning, somewhat belatedly, to catch up on her reading. She read about Donald Trump and learned about the millions his father had made in real estate and construction. And she learned that Donald was already a rich man in his own right—at least he and his father together had holdings that made them multimillionaires. She found that he was beginning to be noticed by the media as a celebrity and a man who might be going places.

"Ivana realized that there wasn't any question but that her future would be very well-established if she married Donald," Morris said. "He had a real future in real estate."

And Ivana discussed the situation with Yolande Cardinal as well. She did not want to hurt George Syrovatka, but it was becoming obvious with each passing day that she would be making a final and irrevocable decision soon—and when it was done, something that had been bright and shining in her life would be bleak and extinguished.

The two men were so different—but so much the same.

The two men's families were different, too. Ivana had known the Syrovatkas for years. She had just met Donald Trump's family. He had taken her to New York and invited her over to the house where his family lived. That in itself was an unusual thing for Donald Trump to do. He did not bring home women he met at casual affairs.

He wanted her to see that his was a closely-knit family. According to Cardinal, he knew how hard it had been for Ivana to give up her own family—another closely-knit one—to go to Canada to live. He knew she felt the need for a good family life in her future. The Trumps had that: they were family oriented. "For Ivana that was great, because she didn't have a family here, and she's an only child."

With Donald Trump, Ivana could see that she would have a nice family that was all together and very, very close. "Family was important to her," Cardinal said.

In her brief talks with Donald Trump, Cardinal heard him say once that he was positive he would never marry a New Yorker. He said the reason for his prejudice against them was that he always suspected they might be after his money.

In New York it was axiomatic that any man with money was a moving target for women. Donald Trump was wealthy and the women were all aware of how much money there was to get.

That was the reason he did not trust them. But he came to trust Ivana—not because she did not know about his money; after all, she did—but because he could see what kind of a person she really was. In fact, in an odd way, he felt that she was the mirror image of him.

But Donald was a very thorough person. In his business deals, he always got his homework done before he made a move. He spent a lot more time in investigative work about a project before making a decision than most of his contemporaries. He was the same with women.

He continued to find out all he could about Ivana—from her friends, as well as from her. He would talk with Yolande Cardinal, and then call Audrey Morris, and chat about Ivana and about her life in Canada. He even at one point told Morris he was interested in Ivana.

He told her about himself, too; about his plans, about his self-assessment. "I'm either going to make it and make a lot of money, but I could lose it overnight," he admitted to her. Morris understood what he meant. She was a businesswoman herself, and she knew the rules of the game—namely, that there really weren't any.

"He was straightforward," she said. But Morris understood something about Donald Trump that Ivana did not know at that time. "Donald was really looking for a wife. He was a very confident man, and he knew exactly what he wanted in the way of a wife. He told me that he had been out with a number of very beautiful ladies, but when he spotted Ivana, he knew that she was the one."

It was during these chats that Donald Trump got what he called a second opinion about Ivana.

"Once Donald called me and asked me flat out what my impressions of Ivana were. I gave it to him straight from the hip. I told him exactly what I felt about her. I told him that she was one of my very top models and I respected her very highly."

Donald told her that he felt the same way and that Morris's assessment had just confirmed his own feelings about her.

"Donald had been out with many Eileen Ford models, and a fashion model can be somewhat pretentious. When you take off the beautiful makeup and the lovely clothes, sometimes they're very shallow. Donald was looking for something more than outward beauty. He was looking for someone highly intelligent because he had his plan then of what he was going to do with the rest of his life."

He was searching now for character and attitude, as well as intelligence, in the woman he would share his life with. He wanted someone who would fit in with him when he began to make it to the top—as, of course, he had always known he would.

There was not a great deal of discussion between Ivana and Morris about Ivana's important decision—to choose between a future with George Syrovatka or a future with Donald Trump—but there was enough. It was obvious to those closest to her that Ivana was trying to make up her mind in the very fairest way possible, given the circumstances.

There was no way to make any decision without badly hurting someone. George had been responsible for getting Ivana out of Czechoslovakia. Donald would be responsible for setting up Ivana in New York. If she chose Donald, she would hurt George. If she chose George, she would hurt Donald.

Ivana knew that she owed a great deal to George. "It had been a very long friendship—her relationship with him—and they both spoke the same language, had the same food habits, shared everything," Cardinal said. "George meant a lot to Ivana."

Again and again in her mind, she went back to George. Without him, Ivana would never have made good in Montreal, without him, she would certainly have been a lesser person.

Could she leave him now to take up a new and unknown future with someone she had just met?

In spite of the weather in Aspen, the relationship between Ivana and Donald had heated up a considerable degree. The time was fast coming when Ivana would have to make up her mind about her future. Was it going to be with George? Or was it going to be with Donald?

Morris knew that a crisis was fast approaching. She could tell by Ivana's attitude. "Ivana must have been torn," she said, "because George was a very fine man and a good skier, whom she liked, and she lived with George in his very lovely apartment. When she met Donald and started seeing him frequently, she came to a point where she had to make her decision."

Meanwhile, in New York, the Trump family was following all these moves with the same intensity that Ivana's friends were following them in Montreal. The Trumps saw Ivana for what she was, a competitor and a woman with her own destiny solidly in control. There was no question but that Fred Trump approved of this svelte, controlled, self-assured young woman.

After all, he knew she had come from a solid middle-class background, the same as his. She, like her father, was a sensible person with both feet on the ground. She had grown up in an atmosphere where hard work and persistence were rewarded— especially in her interest in sports. And he sensed that she was a family person, not a swinger or airhead jet-setter. Fred Trump recognized in her the same qualities of character he had tried to instill in his own children.

Certainly Donald's mother, with her Scottish background of thrift, work, and family, understood Ivana from the beginning. She knew that her son was intelligent, but she did not know how knowledgeable he might be about women. She had always feared that he might become attracted to a woman who would not be good for him. She felt that Ivana was the right person.

The parents watched with amusement as the rather short court-ship got underway in the fall and winter of 1976-1977. They liked Ivana and they waited for the inevitable to happen. Fred Trump put it this way:

"Donald folded up like an umbrella the first time he saw her."

And they knew it was a serious match when Donald started regularly taking his private limousine to the airport to pick up Ivana when she made one of her increasingly frequent weekend visits to New York.

There was no question about it. Ivana was intrigued. Intrigued and—hooked. In a way, a future with Donald Trump was even more than she had ever expected out of life. She had made a good thing out of her move to Canada, had succeeded both in her skiing career and in the highly competitive world of modeling. She was now about to stand on her own two feet financially, and could mold her future into anything she wanted it to be.

Through her own talent and daring, she had opted to take on life in a brand new country and a strange new culture—and she had tamed it to her liking. And now, here was a man who could wave a magic wand at her and transform her from a middle-class professional model and sportsperson into a fairy queen—an ice maiden out of the tales of Hans Christian Andersen.

Things were moving ahead. In January Donald asked Ivana to marry him, and when she gave her answer in the affirmative, he presented her with a ring. They were officially engaged—almost a quaint thing in the 1970s. The engagement ring was beautiful—an oval diamond of about five carats.

It is not known exactly when Ivana cleared the way for her engagement to Donald Trump, but it is known that she did confront George finally about what was happening to their foundering relationship.

"She decided finally that George was not what she was looking for," was the way Yolande Cardinal put it in trying to describe what happened between Ivana and George. This was the final confrontation between two people who had shared a life together for five years in Canada and another five in Czechoslovakia. It was not an easy parting.

George had, of course, found out about the sudden appearance of Donald Trump in Ivana's life. At first he seemed astounded that Ivana had the nerve to be going out with someone else when the two of them, he thought, were so happy together.

At this point, it seems evident that Ivana once again brought up the crucial point of marriage. It is assumed that she told George once again that she was the type of person who wanted a family, close ties, marriage.

And so the serious discussion of her future with George took place. Her several friends learned from Ivana what happened.

"She wanted to get married to George," Cardinal said. "She wanted children and a family. George was not mature enough or ready for that at all. It was the wrong timing."

It had been a very long friendship, and a very important one to both of them, but Ivana decided that it was a relationship that was not ever going to be what she had been looking for all her life.

Ivana said, "If you feel ready for marriage, great. I'm always ready to get married, have children, and raise a family."

But George did not feel ready for marriage at that time. Whatever happened between the two of them, Ivana made the final decision, and, after talking over the possibilities with George— and presumably finding that his answer to marriage was still no— she packed her belongings and moved out.

And by moving out, she left open the possibility that Donald Trump might indeed ask her to marry him. Which, of course, he did.

It was very hard for the two of them. And yet it was a friendly parting. When Ivana went, she left the door open for George, if he decided to change his mind.

"She felt very torn about making a final split with George," Monique Clement said. "They had been childhood sweethearts, they had a common background, she had cared for him very much, and even though the relationship was no longer satisfying probably to either of them, it's always difficult to leave a relationship, and the fact that she was already interested in somebody else probably made her feel doubly guilty."

But, guilty or not, she made the move.

According to Cardinal, she felt that George was not the type ever to get serious about marriage. She said he liked groups and liked having fun. As for taking on big responsibilities—no way.

In truth, the exact time of the breakup is not known. Morris believes it was shortly after Ivana met Donald. On the other hand, Cardinal is under the impression that the breakup occurred before Ivana met Donald.

But by the time Ivana accepted Donald's engagement ring, the decision had been made and George and Ivana were through. The Trump family celebrated the announcement first. And then

Ivana and Donald traveled to Montreal, where she showed off her new ring to her small circle of friends.

"Ivana seemed very excited, but more than that, she was so madly in love with Donald," Morris related. About the two of them, she said, "there was an incredible chemistry, an aura around them both. They seemed to be melting. She had no question at that time in her mind that he was the right man."

"Ivana's got a very, very practical streak in her," Yolande Cardinal said. "When she met Donald Trump, she realized that he was what she had been looking for—a good husband."

But of course, she would never forget George. "He was part of her childhood, her Czech past." Cardinal said they remained "very good friends" even after Ivana moved out.

Meanwhile, George had somehow gotten the bad news. He did not take it well. "He was pretty shocked to find out she was going to marry somebody else," George's brother Michael said. After all, George had presumed that Ivana would be coming back to him in due course. "He was pretty unhappy for a while. I remember driving with him in the car. He was driving pretty fast, aggressive, reckless."

The breakup, according to Michael, was not all that friendly. But, after all, he had always wondered how long things would last between his brother George and Ivana.

"I thought she was spoiled," Michael recalled, "and I just kind of distanced myself. I obviously thought she wasn't good enough for George. I always had the impression that she was a spoiled brat. She would want to have her way, and it would be her way or the highway. She would act insulted, or sulk. She was smart: If she wanted something, she knew how to get it."

And that did not make her the right companion for his brother. "George is easygoing, and Ivana knew how to manipulate him to get her way. She was the only child and she was used to it that everything she wanted, she always got."

Michael said that he remembered that his brother was still living with Ivana at the time she took up with Donald. "She moved down to New York, then came back to get her things two or three months later. She had a car in Montreal; she went down to New York, and then she came back to get her car."

After the engagement party in New York and the subsequent

trip to Montreal, the newly-engaged couple began shuttling back and forth between Montreal and New York on weekends.

"They were very much in love with each other," Cardinal remembered. "Donald was exactly what Ivana wanted—a mature man who was ready to get married and who wanted to raise a family. Ivana loved children, and she knew that it was very important for her to have more than one."

To Audrey Morris, the relationship between Ivana and Donald Trump seemed ordained from the beginning, and from the moment they met, the future seemed orchestrated for an adagio. "They courted, they engaged, and they married—all within a fairly short time," she said. "It was that old cliché—a whirlwind romance." A summer through spring fait accompli.

And yet, and yet . . .

Ivana's friend Monique Clement thought that Ivana and Donald were rushing things just a bit. She was conscious that Ivana, before the wedding to Donald, was not quite herself.

"I remember her being afraid because it was so very fast. Basically the normal jitters of 'Oh, my God, this is so sudden, and it's scary because he has money and this is a fast type of life.' He was very much rushing it. She did not chase this man. She was almost reluctant."

But nothing was going to stop this juggernaut once it got rolling.

Ivana Zelnickova and Donald Trump were married on April 9, 1977, at Marble Collegiate Church on Fifth Avenue in New York City by Norman Vincent Peale, long a firm friend of the Trump family, and the obvious man to perform the ceremony. It was, in fact, a very quiet wedding, beautiful but intimate, restricted to the immediate family and a very few close friends.

Ivana wore a two-piece chiffon full-skirted off-the-shoulder dress with full sleeves, according to Audrey Morris, who was present. "It was waltz-length, mid-calf and quite simple—totally ornamented with a long veil, but no train." It was designed by one of the most famous designers in Canada, according to Yolande Cardinal, who was also present.

The setting was perfect for the perfect fairy-tale wedding, according to Morris. "As soon as we entered the church, there was this wonderful perfume coming from those beautiful blossoms that filled the upper balcony. It was Easter season, and the entire front of the church was full of thousands of Easter lilies—all in white. It was quite magnificent."

The ceremony was a traditional Protestant one, lasting about half an hour. Everyone was dressed in black tie and long gowns. Donald's two sisters, Maryanne and Elizabeth, were bridesmaids, and his brothers, Fred and Robert, the best man and usher. There were also flower girls who wore pink dresses and flowers in their hair.

Even though the ceremony was simple, Ivana was uncharacteristically nervous. Audrey Morris was surprised at her frame of mind.

"I was in Donald's apartment when she was dressing, and I saw how nervous she was." To Morris, it was obvious why Ivana was unnerved. "She didn't know many of the people there, and this was a very big step in her life—she was entering into New York society, marrying a young man who was from a very well-known family." Well, at least well-known in the real-estate world.

But to make it happier for Ivana, her parents had come to the wedding from Czechoslovakia. "They were very emotional," Cardinal said, explaining: "Their only child was getting married, and so far away from home." Mayor Edward Koch was present, giving the wedding ceremony a very special New York flavor. Koch doffed a ceremonial hat to the Trumps, whom he at that time revered.

"Were you nervous? Were you scared to death?" a television interviewer asked her many years later.

"Good enough," responded Ivana. She meant, "Scared enough."

"But no second thoughts, right?"

"No second thoughts. Just very nervous."

"Was [Donald] nervous?"

"I don't know. I'm not sure."

After the wedding, there was a reception at Twenty-One, with a sitdown dinner and dancing afterwards. It went on until about three o'clock in the morning.

"Ivana was nervous because she didn't know anyone," Cardinal said. "It was hard on her."

But she survived. And so did her friends and parents. In fact, Audrey Morris reported that both Ivana and Donald "were so gracious to me. Donald provided me with his silver-gray limousine for four days."

By that time, of course, the newlyweds were some thousands of miles away—in Acapulco, Mexico—celebrating their honeymoon.

George Syrovatka kept visiting Jay Peak in Vermont on weekends, taking with him a number of girlfriends, among them Monique Clement, who had been a friend of Ivana's.

In 1980, the Jay Peak instructors built a downhill race and named it after George—calling it the George Syrovatka International Downhill.

And every year George would go out and set the pace for the run.

George married Monique Clement eventually, they had a son, and then the two of them were divorced.

"George skis almost every weekend at Jay," Mickey Doheney said recently, "and his son is in our junior program."

Chapter Six
The Grand Face-Lift

Although the next few years were a time of settling in for Ivana Trump, they were in no way very placid ones. Almost from the moment the Trumps returned from their extended honeymoon in Acapulco, her life became a whirlwind of activity.

Because Donald was so busy with his business engagements, the Trumps had little time to spend looking around for a place to live.

Instead, Ivana moved immediately in with her husband at his large bachelor digs at Olympic Towers at 641 Fifth Avenue. The apartment was spare, but capacious, and Ivana was moved in without any of the usual newlywed-wife troubles.

Looking back on it later, she realized it was a good thing that she had come from healthy physical stock and that her early training in sports activities had taught her how to pace herself. For life with Donald Trump was not laid-back. It was typically in overdrive.

During their courting months, Ivana had been with him during his weekends, and, while they had been fun-filled times, the hours had frequently been interrupted with phone calls, meetings, and protracted business negotiations. And so Ivana had been initiated into the kind of life style that she would soon become an integral part of.

Yet once she was involved in it, she found it a problem to keep up with the man whom she now called "The Donald." The use of the article in front of the Christian name may sound quaint to an American ear, but there is a very logical reason for it.

Czechoslovakian is a language without articles—the or a. It is difficult for Czechs to learn languages that have articles. Once they get into the swing of English, they tend to add articles to everything, almost as a matter of course.

"The Donald" seemed quite fitting to Ivana's mind; he was the only Donald in her life.

And he was the most important Donald in the lives of many other people—as was attested to by the number of phone calls he was apt to receive during an ordinary dinner at home. It was a rare Saturday night meal that was not interrupted by at least a half dozen telephone calls—every single one of them crucial.

Busy, busy, busy. The Donald was busy. Ivana was busy. If she still held any cherished notions that she would be able to continue her modeling career, they were soon shattered.

She told a friend once that she had gotten just what she desired in life when she married Donald Trump—just what she desired, with a few minor but important exceptions:

"I wanted a man who was dominant, someone who was very successful in business, someone I could respect. When I first married Donald it was very rough that first year. I got pregnant, I quit my job in Montreal, I totally gave up my modeling career, and every day in New York Donald was introducing me to about a thousand people. I didn't think I would be able to take it."

Ivana never thought her life as Mrs. Trump would be a series of afternoon teas and bridge games with the society ladies of Manhattan, but even so, Donald Trump's demanding pace was just a bit more than she had bargained for. She had anticipated that he would want to show off his new bride to all his friends and associates.

Her only miscalculation was in estimating the very large number of these acquaintances. The Trumps went everywhere. They saw everyone. It was exhausting, it was breathtaking, it was—marvelous.

The first year of married life was a memorable one for each of the newlyweds.

For Ivana, she had found a dominant man to mold her life into something exciting and rewarding.

For Donald, he had found an intelligent, beautiful, and energetic wife who could almost run the course as well as he could.

Within that first eventful, revolutionary year of their marriage, Ivana gave birth to a baby boy. Inevitably, the boy was named Donald J. Trump, Jr. Ivana took giving birth in stride, as she took almost everything else—including Donald Trump.

Kathie Lee Gifford once discussed having babies with Ivana, asking the following lead-in question to open up the conversation:

"But you did take off a lot of time when your children were very young, didn't you?"

"I really never took time off," Ivan corrected her. "No."

"You didn't?"

"I would give the births and I would be in my office two days later."

"Two days?" Kathie Lee was appalled. "Thanks a lot, Ivana!"

Sugar Rautbord, a writer who became a good friend of Ivana's in the 1970s through mutual acquaintances, knew all about Ivana's casual attitude toward birth, and admired it immensely.

She put it this way:

"The night before Ivana gave birth to her first child, she was out dancing and looking magnificent. I thought that was most remarkable. She wasn't even wearing a maternity dress!"

But then, Ivana had always been reticent about discussing all personal subjects, in addition to babies and bringing up children.

For example, no one was ever able to pin her down on her actual feelings for Donald Trump.

Regis Philbin and Kathie Lee Gifford once tried very hard to get Ivana's first impression of Donald Trump.

All they got was this:

"How did you meet him, exactly?" Regis asked her, referring to Donald Trump. "Where and when and why?"

Silence from Ivana.

Kathie picked up the ball. "It sounds like an advertisement, doesn't it?"

Finally Ivana murmured: "It's very private, but it's very personal."

Regis waved his hands. "Oh, is it! Oh, is it? I didn't know that."

Kathie smiled. "That means it was fabulous." She turned to Regis with a mocking look. "And it's none of your business."

"Did he sneak into your room one night?" Regis wondered impishly.

"No!" snapped Ivana. "Not that personal, not that personal."

"But he must have pursued you. You are gorgeous, blonde, a beautiful model—"

"No," said Ivana coolly. "He tried his best. What Donald wants, Donald gets—right?"

Kathie nodded. "Yes."

"Right. He gets. And then he proposed?" Regis asked persistently.

"Uh-huh."

"And you accepted?"

"Yes."

And that was all the dross they got by mining Ivana's romantic vein.

Meanwhile, Ivana was busy not only preparing for her first birth, but also finding and furnishing a larger, more airy apartment further up Fifth Avenue—a building simply called 800—to which they would soon move.

Ivana hired an interior decorator named Barbara Greene, of G. K. R. Associates, to help her learn about the art of interior decoration for the Trumps' coming move.

The apartment building overlooking Central Park at Sixty-second Street was fairly small in comparison to other large apartments in New York—it encompassed about eight rooms—but it was nicely put together and very pleasant for Ivana to furnish. She found that she loved to put things together in a new way.

In fact, Donald Trump was prompted once to describe to a friend his wife's "impeccable taste and her imagination and flair" in matters of interior decoration. Although Ivana was unaware of it at the time—and so, for that matter was Donald—she would soon be called on to use that flair to help her husband in one of his most important business projects to date.

In those rather busy, but definitely happy, months of her life in their new apartment, Ivana was able to indulge herself as most new wives do; with time spent on her baby son, with time spent on the decorating and furnishings, with time spent on cooking a bit, and with time spent on playing with their black poodle, called Tlapka, which is Czechoslovakian for paw.

"When I got her thirteen years ago," Ivana explained, "she was just a puppy, and she had hurt one foot somehow. Donald— he just tolerates her."

Ivana confessed that she had soon lost interest in whipping up a Czechoslovakian specialty for her husband. Twice a week she took over cooking the dinner. "I was doing all kinds of beautiful sauces," she said, "but Donald only eats steaks and potatoes, so I gave up."

Even so, by 1979, Ivana was mistress of at least three residences: one in Aspen, Colorado, where the Trumps would both go for long weekends during the skiing season; one in Wainscott, on Long Island, where they spent long weekends in the summer months; and their town house in Manhattan overlooking Central Park.

Ivana could say, in all honesty, that their social life was low-keyed in the summer. "We don't give our phone number to many people. We don't give parties. And we accept invitations from only very close friends."

When Audrey Morris visited the Fifth Avenue apartment, she recalled: "Ivana did the interior design in that apartment. I remember her dining room distinctly; it had not one but two pewter gray oval tables. If she was having a small, intimate party, she could use one table. And if she had a large group, she could use two. The baby's room was also unique—Ivana had designed the furniture built into the corner, in an interesting steps-and-stairs configuration."

But the domestic bliss indicated here was not to last very long. Ivana Trump was about to be called in to help her husband's business enterprises in a way she had never dreamed she might be involved.

Donald Trump had taken part in the campaign that Hugh L. Carey successfully waged in 1974 for the governorship of New York. Both Donald and his father had contributed generously to Carey's election. In his work for Carey, Trump met a woman named Louise M. Sunshine, who was chairperson of Carey's campaign finance committee. Donald was impressed by her ability not only to raise money, but to accomplish just about anything she set her mind on. She was, as he saw it, a go-getter just like him.

At the end of the successful campaign, Donald Trump hired her to work for the Trump Organization on a political level—in other words, to lobby for the Trumps in Albany on a statewide basis. At about the same time, Donald was rewarded for his help in electing Carey by being appointed to the state housing commission.

With Louise Sunshine's help, the Trump Organization persuaded New York City officials in December 1975 to build a new convention center on the nine blocks of property formerly owned by the Penn Central Railroad. Donald Trump sold the property on which he had the option to the Viban Development Corporation for $12,000,000. For the sale, he received a half million dollars in commission, plus $88,000 in expenses. What he wanted was for the city to name the new convention center after his father, Fred Trump. He said later that he would have waived his $88,000 in expenses if they had done so, but the offer was refused. Unfortunately, the convention center became bogged down in huge cost overruns and foundered for several years before finally moving ahead to completion in the 1980s.

But now Donald turned his attention to a new project—this one a renovation rather than a construction deal. Note that he had not yet actually built anything in New York. He had wheeled and dealed, but had contributed nothing in the way of a single building to the island of Manhattan.

The new renovation project was typical Trump. When everyone in New York considered real estate a disaster, Trump decided to buy property, improve it, and sell it. This time the target was located on a site right in the middle of town that was dying of neglect, disuse, and creeping poverty.

Trump told the story in his autobiography. It all started sometime late in 1974, he recalled, when he was chatting with Victor Palmieri.

"What other properties does the Penn Central own that I can buy for nothing?" Trump asked him—half-kidding, half-serious.

Palmieri raised an eyebrow. "As a matter of fact we do have some hotels you might be interested in."

Hotels? The Penn Central owned four hotels that were only a stone's throw from one another, right in the neighborhood of Grand Central Station. In alphabetical order they were the Barclay, the Biltmore, the Commodore, and the Roosevelt. A quick look at the four properties was an eye-opener for Donald Trump. The Barclay, the Biltmore, and the Roosevelt (named for Teddy, not F.D.R.) were obviously alive and well, but the Commodore . . .

It was already half in ruins. Grand Central Station was only then beginning to become the temporary shelter for the thousands of homeless soon to congregate in the city. At that time, the Commodore was on its last legs. Store fronts around it were boarded up. Bag ladies patrolled its lobby. Derelicts slept nearby in the station. The hotel lobby was dingy and rundown.

A brief investigative flurry into the city's books showed Trump that the hotel had been losing a million and a half dollars every year for several years running.

As he stood there one day, doing a characteristic Donald Trump on-site survey of the property, he suddenly became aware of one of those anomalies that exist in New York City. While the transients snored in filthy disarray against the walls, thousands of well-dressed, well-off, trendy commuters stepped over them on their way to Wall Street or Madison Avenue.

The site was perfect, Donald reasoned. What was on the site was a disgrace. And he made one of his quick decisions. He was going to buy that hotel, fix it up, and sell it. And he was determined he would sell it for a very good price.

What was more, he did so. This is the way he worked it out.

First, he told Palmieri that he wanted to buy the Commodore, but at as low a figure as possible. At the same time, he had to convince Palmieri that *he* was the one to sell it to—and not someone else. And he had to keep Palmieri's interest without putting up any money.

Secondly, he had to interest a buyer in helping him to purchase the hotel and renovate it. He had to interest a buyer who would be willing to take over and maintain the new hotel in spite of its rundown site. Not an easy task.

And yet, because the city of New York was in such desperate financial straits—for example, the Commodore owed six million dollars in back taxes to the city—Donald Trump felt it might be possible to get some kind of a tax break to help underwrite the project he was hoping to initiate. It was easy to point out that the six million would be lost unless someone took over and rejuvenated the hotel.

The deal Trump wanted to make went like this:

Trump would take out an option to purchase the hotel for six million dollars, on the proviso that he get tax abatement, financing, and a buying partner. To cement the deal, Trump would put down $250,000 in cash to Penn Central for the exclusive option to purchase.

But before he parted company with any of the quarter million dollars in hard cash, Trump wanted to complete the deal—namely, to find a partner and to negotiate a tax break from the city. And, before he could get a partner, he had to have a scenario that would interest a buyer in purchasing the property.

That meant getting down on paper a workable renovation plan that would make the cost look worthwhile.

For this sensitive but pivotal task, Donald selected a young architect with the unlikely name of Der Scutt. Scutt liked Donald's idea, and went to work with enthusiasm—on spec—following as well as he could Trump's basic scheme of producing a brand-new look.

What intrigued Trump was Seagram's Tower on Park Avenue. Why not use bronze instead of the tired brick of the Commodore? Or even glass? Trump's taste was glitzy and dramatic; he wanted something that would make people stop and stare.

In his business dealings with Der Scutt, Donald Trump did not let friendship or personality stand in the way of getting the very best from the money he put out. "I love quality," Donald said once, "but I don't believe in paying top price for quality."

When Donald originally hired his architect to draw up plans for the proposed Grand Hyatt Hotel, Der Scutt was working for a large architectural firm named Kahn & Jacobs/Hellmuth, Obata & Kassabaum. In April 1975, however, Scutt called and told Donald that he had been fired from his job. This put Donald in a quandary. He could not afford to work with Scutt as an individual; he needed the prestige of a big firm behind the plans he was having drawn up.

Within weeks Scutt formed an association with another firm called Gruzen & Partners. And now Donald went to work. Because the Obata group wanted to keep the job, as did Der Scutt too, Donald was able to negotiate a much lower architectural fee by playing them off against one another.

Donald admitted that in the end he paid Der Scutt "a very modest fee." (Read: a pittance.) But, of course, he pointed out that Scutt's work on the hotel would be the making of him. "Der wasn't thrilled about his fee," Donald admitted. Quality—but at bargain basement rates. That was Donald's modus operandi. And it worked.

While Scutt worked up a set of blueprints, Trump went shopping around for a buying partner. He had always liked the Hyatt Hotel chain's image—glossy, glitzy, but clean and light. Hyatt also favored accommodating conventions; the Grand Central Station site would be perfect for them. Besides, Hyatt had no big hotel in New York.

"I'd heard they wanted one someday," Trump said. Perhaps they did, but it was Donald Trump who made them do something about it. Finding his way eventually to Jay Pritzker, whose family owned a controlling interest in the company, and who ran the Hyatt chain, Donald managed to work out a partnership deal that he considered favorable.

It went like this: Trump and the Hyatt organization would be equal partners in this one project. Trump would build the hotel and Hyatt would manage it when it was operable.

On May 4, 1975, the partners announced that they would purchase, gut, and rebuild the Commodore—if they could get financing and tax abatement.

By this time, Donald Trump was well aware that his father was not at all happy with this scheme. "I told Donald that buying the Commodore at a time when even the Chrysler Building was in receivership was like fighting for a seat on the *Titanic*. But he insisted."

And for a time it seemed that Fred was right and Donald was wrong.

Not only were Trump and Hyatt unable to get bank financing, but the city sat tight, refusing to extend any tax abatement at all. Nevertheless, they were finally able to sit down and hammer out an arrangement of sorts.

Trump and Hyatt would buy the Commodore from Penn Central for ten million dollars, six million of which would go to the city to pay the back taxes. Then Trump and Hyatt would sell the hotel for one dollar to New York state's Urban Development Corporation; the UDC would lease it back to Trump for ninety-nine years. Trump's rent, in lieu of property taxes, would start at $250,000 a year, and rise in the fortieth year to $2.7 million. And Trump would pay the city a percentage of the profits.

Trump eventually got financing from the Equitable Life Assurance Society and the Bronx Savings Bank.

No one was quiet when the final details were revealed to the public via the various media. Many competitors bled openly in front of the television cameras. Others stated their disdain in writing. Still others simply started talking to anyone who would listen.

"Clearly, the city could be getting a better deal," said Deputy Mayor Robert F. Wagner, Jr. "But Donald Trump made his deal at a time when the city was desperate for development. Also, he had the vision to have picked the Commodore site when he did. You've got to remember that when Trump bought the Commodore, East Forty-second Street was going downhill, and nobody was building hotels in New York."

One disgruntled member of the City Council, Henry J. Stern, said: "Donald Trump runs with the same clique that continues to manipulate things behind the scenes in this city. He has ties through his father to the Brooklyn Democratic machine that produced Hugh Carey. Roy Cohn is his lawyer. He throws around a lot of money in political campaigns."

As for Donald Trump, he spoke in this fashion: "The city's a disaster. Everyone believes it's going to get worse. But I'm the only one who believes the opposite. I'm the only one who's willing to buy the Commodore."

"Yes," snapped back a writer for *Barron's*. "But why is the city willing to give you a forty-year tax abatement?"

And then came the punchline, one that might seem to have been almost tailor-made for the film *Wall Street* some ten years later: "Because I didn't ask for fifty," said Donald Trump.

In 1969 the hard hats moved in with their heavy equipment and went to work on the Commodore Hotel. Dust rose, plaster drifted, lumber split, and huge sections of walls and floor fell to the ground. In the pit created, the demolition experts steadily ground up the remains and boxed it into crates to be hauled away and dumped in the ground somewhere.

The end of the Commodore was in sight. But at the same time, a new beginning for Forty-second Street and the center of New York City was in the offing. Whether or not it would be a success was moot. Moot to everyone perhaps but Donald Trump. He knew it was a new beginning—and a successful one to boot.

"I could have saved millions and millions of dollars just by refurbishing the old Commodore rather than by creating a brand-new building." Not Donald Trump. "The Chrysler Building is in foreclosure, the neighborhood is a disaster, and it's obvious something's not working. If you think I'm going to leave the facade of the old Commodore the way it is, you're crazy. There's no way."

Design-wise, Donald Trump was what might be called a lobby man. To him, it was the entryway to a hotel or a building that set its essential tone. If the lobby was dramatic and appealing, he could move forward with a happy stride. If the lobby was grim or somehow dull, he was frankly down on the whole place.

"Most hotel lobbies in New York are dull and unexciting," was the way he saw it.

And so with Der Scutt, he managed an unforgettable and eye-appealing lobby for his new structure. The lobby itself is at least four stories in height, with several levels immediately visible to the naked eye. In addition, there is a 170-foot glass-enclosed restaurant pitched out over the sidewalk on Forty-second Street. Oddly enough, no one had done that kind of thing before in New York.

There is a live waterfall in the center of the lobby, right by the escalators. In the lobby itself are two restaurants, with three others nearby.

So much for the design.

It is the materials that went into the construction of Der Scutt's exciting plan that really made it work.

And here Donald Trump got help from an unexpected source. That source was Ivana Trump. In decorating their new apartment on Central Park, she had exhibited an eye for exciting things, for materials that appealed. At least, they appealed to Donald.

He appointed her Vice President in charge of Interior Decorating for the Trump Organization. And she reveled in the job. Although Donald Trump was always there to okay her decisions, it was she who had the most to say about the materials, about the color schemes, and about the designs that went into the new hotel.

Ivana Trump had no idea if she was an expert or not, but she knew what she wanted. With her, a decision was more or less simply a gut feeling. Ivana intuitively went in for the dramatic, exactly the same way her husband did. Sometimes her taste tended to be a bit tacky, or a bit glitzy, or even grossly *schlock*— but somehow, in concert with everything else, it worked. That was what counted.

Ivana herself once said it. "I know what I like. There is no wallpaper, no fabric, no lacquer, no carpet, no marble in any of our buildings that didn't get my approval. Then, of course, I bring it to my husband, for his approval."

For example, the floor of the Hyatt lobby—the hotel was renamed the Grand Hyatt as a concession to Grand Central Station during the construction—is laid in beautiful *paradiso* marble. The railings and columns are made of brass, not chrome or nickel.

It was Ivana herself who selected the brownish-pink *paradiso* marble. She also selected the walnut paneling that makes up the visible walls, the bronze columns, the gold handrails, the golden-brown velours, and the weird giant metalwork mobile that lurks in the sitting area in front of the elevators. And she helped change the shape of the one-step waterfall originally proposed into a multilevel affair.

To assist her in choosing certain materials and combinations of material for the Grand Hyatt, Ivana constantly sought out the advice of her old mentor, Barbara Greene.

Ivana loved the work. She would leave the Fifth Avenue apartment about ten o'clock in the morning, and drop over to Forty-second Street to see to anything that had to be tended to. With Mrs. Greene, she would execute a complete walkaround of the site, and by noon she would attend her thrice-weekly exercise class, or her twice-weekly hairdressing appointment. She would be home by four P.M., to greet her masseuse.

"I have to look pretty and fresh," she told *The New York Times*, which had just discovered her existence, "because we have to entertain people so much."

As for working with her husband, she admitted to the press that she would love to work outside the family. But "Donald's afraid that if I go back to work now I'll get so involved that I won't have another child."

She said that Donald would like to have five children.

"He'll get maybe two or three," she added with a quick smile. It is to be noted that indeed Ivana was never to be deterred from her own mind-set on that subject.

Whether she tailored herself to adhere to The Donald's tastes, or whether she inherently saw things exactly the same way as her husband, Ivana triumphantly carried out the extremely modern concept of design that so fascinated Donald Trump.

"This is the way I help Donald," Ivana said. "All the details to worry about. If I can do these little things, he knows he can trust me totally, and then he can spend his time on the more important things."

In fact, she was a constant presence at the construction site. With the hard hat pulled down over her freshly-coiffed hair, and overalls fitting her body snugly, she would stroll about the area, talking to the electricians, the plumbers, the carpenters, and the steelworkers, waving her brilliantly painted fingernails in all directions.

"This is not the right color. You have to move this stripe. I want this screw moved over there. The wall must be moved over here."

They would howl in revolt. Ivana's close friend, Sugar Rautbord, once pointed out: "But Ivana was right. It worked. It looked great. It was just what both the Trumps wanted. And it wasn't as if Ivana asked people to work when she was not there. She worked right alongside the rest of them."

Yes, she drove them crazy. Yet it was impossible to contradict her because if anyone did, he or she would be immediately reprimanded from higher headquarters and told to obey or else.

What concerned Ivana the most was the time element in the construction schedule. She knew that the most costly area in any construction job was overtime; she knew it because Donald drummed the fact into her incessantly. The idea was to get the job done quickly and get it done right. Ivana, like Donald, was a fanatic about time.

"When will it be finished?" she would ask an electrician about an outlet. "When can I tell him"—Donald Trump—"it will be done?"

There was the story of the worker who failed to show up one day because, very simply, he was busy somewhere else. But Ivana would not accept his nonappearance with a silly excuse like that. She went after the man unmercifully.

"After she leaves the site I always have a thousand new things to do!" he complained to his boss. "You can never satisfy Mrs. Trump!"

"I put on this tough act because if you say 'please, please' to these guys, the job will never get done the way we want it done." So said Ivana Trump in answer to the worker's complaint.

Ivana Trump's involvement with construction, decoration, and management (eventually) came about more or less as a pure fluke.

"When I married Ivana," Donald Trump said, "I had no intention of working with her, but she has a great abundance of talent, and it was natural to put that talent to work."

"We work as a team," Ivana said. "Donald has the vision of what he'd like to own, and he usually ends up owning it. Once that happens, I often become the manager. Donald is lucky I can manage, and I am lucky he gives me the chance."

Ivana once explained how her work with her husband affected her own life style. "Donald and I have the pressure of being known. We're always on display. It can be hard to balance work, our family, and our social life. We enjoy the social life, but we like to stay home and have a private life, too."

The Grand Hyatt was completed and opened in September 1980. It was indeed a brand-new property. It had around fourteen hundred rooms, a presidential suite renting at two thousand dollars a night, a ballroom, a shopping arcade, and five restaurants. And it was a smash hit from the start. Soon it was grossing thirty million dollars a year.

But Donald Trump had never been a hands-off person. Nor had Ivana been. Trump related a story about Ivana in his autobiography.

Several months after the Grand Hyatt was open, he had a telephone call from the head of the Hyatt chain. "Donald, we have a problem," Patrick Foley told him. "The manager of the [Grand Hyatt] is going nuts, because your wife comes by, and she'll see dust in the corner of the lobby and call over a porter to clean it up. Or she'll see a doorman in a uniform that's not pressed, and she'll tell him to get it cleaned. Unfortunately, my manager happens to be a guy who has a problem with women to start off with. But, in his defense, he's running a hotel with fifteen hundred employees, and there's got to be a chain of command, or else a business like this just doesn't work."

Nevertheless, Ivana continued to visit the hotel, and the manager continued to fume until the head of the chain finally transferred him elsewhere, and sent in a new manager. Then the problem gradually faded away.

Things had calmed down for Ivana—to the degree to which they could calm down in a family as energetic and frenetic as hers was.

So, the settling in of Ivana Trump was not very prolonged, if indeed it ever existed. Almost at once after her marriage, Ivana Trump joined her husband in his exciting day-to-day activities. He called it negotiating.

"My life," he told *The New York Times*, "is one big negotiation."

These negotiations suited both husband and wife. They worked well together. And it was odd, in a way, that a woman brought up in the tradition of Middle Europe, where wives were helpmates and supporters of their husbands by tradition, religion, and environment; and were never primary movers and shakers, should find herself so aptly suited to diving in and shouldering a great deal of the business burdens of her husband.

She once spoke about working and the work ethic. "I really don't do anything much different than I used to in Czechoslovakia. You know, there, everybody works. And it's the upbringing, you know. I really never knew anything different from working. Everybody works there. I can't sit home and look up at the ceiling. You know, it's in the upbringing that you find out what you do."

Luckily, in Ivana's case, there was plenty to do. No one could guess what she might have been doing if Donald Trump's activities had not fully absorbed her and given her a course of action to follow.

And while the Grand Hyatt was a triumph, it was only a beginning for Donald Trump. A great deal more was yet to come.

Swiftly, too.

Chapter Seven
The Tower That Trump Built

Hardly had the dust settled on the site of the Grand Hyatt with its dramatic opening and its subsequent overnight success as one of the new showplaces of New York City, than Ivana Trump found herself quite happily saddled with a brand-new project to keep her busy.

Once again it had to do with interior decoration. The triumphant reception her handiwork had received from the public was not lost on Donald Trump. Forget about the critics who carped and downgraded the melodrama and the glitz of the Grand Hyatt. It was the people who counted.

Donald Trump decided to keep in mind his wife's expertise with decoration and her meticulous eye for spotting errors and flaws in details of construction work. If he should ever need her help again, he would utilize it.

As for Ivana, she thrived on the work. She developed her natural eye for color and texture into a precision mechanism. Interestingly enough, her taste paralleled Donald's—that is, it too was geared almost exclusively to the dramatic and the eye-catching.

Glittering metals, high ceilings, eye-opening panoramas, glitzy crystal, brilliantly reflecting glass surfaces: these were what she considered, like Donald Trump, arresting and riveting. If at times her taste tended to be just a bit tacky, the total effect nevertheless rarely, if ever, degenerated totally into junk design.

This partnership of creativity with her husband—even if it was just a bit lopsided and weighted on his side—was completely compatible with her idea of what she should be doing with her life. It was especially true now that she was a mother and would in all probability be a mother again.

It was *Town & Country* that pointed out the interesting option that Ivana Trump had settled on in her career/life-style.

"If they chose to, the Trumps could pick up and join the jet set tomorrow," the magazine said. However, "they choose instead to lead a fairly quiet life."

Indeed, when they did go out to dinner in Manhattan, it was usually with just one or two friends. "They go to a handful of restaurants they always enjoy," the magazine reported, listing them as Le Cirque, La Grenouille, Primavera, and Vasata.

Ivana told the magazine that she loved Vasata's wonderful chicken paprika. "And do you know a place called the Duck Joint?" Ivana was referring to an Upper East Side restaurant known for its huge portions. "Oh, I love that place. It's where you can go when you really want to . . ." Finally, she came up with the English expression she was searching for. "Pig-out! Yes!"

Generally speaking, however, the Trumps had not yet chosen to join the jet-setting orbit, with its laid-back millionaires and sophisticated hangers-on. They chose instead to live that so-called quiet life in Manhattan, and get on with their careers—both careers.

And to keep the fires burning, Donald Trump's restless imagination abruptly seized on a new project. And this was one in which he could once again use the talents of his wife. Ivana was at his side ready to assist him in any way she could.

For years Donald Trump had recognized the corner of Fifty-seventh and Fifth Avenue as probably the greatest piece of real estate in Manhattan. And since Manhattan was the absolute center of all action in the business and social world of America, that corner was the best of all possible real-estate sites in the United States. It was no coincidence that within a few feet of that corner stood one of the most exclusive companies in the world—Tiffany's.

The site Donald considered the best was occupied by a department store called Bonwit Teller. Unfortunately, in the late 1970s, Bonwit Teller had come quite suddenly on hard economic times. Ironically, its economic troubles had nothing to do with Bonwit Teller's operation in New York. They had to do with the company that owned Bonwit Teller.

Genesco Inc. had just gone through a financial crisis due to a internecine battle involving a struggle to the death between an angry father and a stubborn son—the father being the original founder of Genesco. This was the organization that had purchased Bonwit Teller's operations. Now, to avert bankruptcy proceedings that might be brought on by its bloody internal battle, the corpo-

The couple seen here at the September 1988 US Open Championships. *(Globe)*

The stunning contrast between Ivana's appearance before and after plastic-surgery. On the right, sporting a new facial look and hairstyle, Donald's "companion" seems years younger. *(Globe)*

The Trumps dancing at the late Malcolm Forbes 70th anniversary in New York, 1987. *(Gamma-Liaison)*

The Trumps with Henry Kravis, CEO of Kravis-Kohlberg who engineered the historic 1989 RJR Nabisco takeover. Seen here at the opening of *The Phantom of the Opera*. *(Gamma-Liaison)*

Marla Maples (in the middle) as winner of the Miss
Hawaiian Tropic Beauty Contest, Daytona Beach, Florida, 1985.
(Gamma-Liaison)

At the March '89 introduction of Joan Collins' new line of perfumes brandnamed "Scoundrel." *(Globe)*

Ivana posing at the Plaza Hotel upon becoming its Director. *(Gamma-Liaison)*

The couple in the lounge of "The Princess." *(Gamma-Liaison)*

August 1989. Ivana with Yasmin Khan, daughter of Rita Hayworth and Ali Khan at the "21 Club." *(Globe)*

Ivana with Marylou, of the famous Whitney family, at a fundraiser for the "March of Dimes" in October 1988. *(Gamma-Liaison)*

Ivana and Donald together on the deck of Trump's "The Princess." The luxury boat formerly belonged to the multi-millionaire and Iranian-born Adnan Khashoggi, now under indictment in New York. *(Gamma-Liaison)*

Marla Maples, on the left, living it up in New York City, July 1989. *(Gamma-Liaison)*

ration appointed a new chairman of the board. His name was John Hanigan.

Hanigan was a hatchet man. His job was to move into a company, cut out the dead wood, sell off all possible assets, get rid of all nonproductive and nonprofitable parts, liquidate as much of it as possible, pay off all the debts, and then sell what was left for a profit, and get out.

Donald Trump sniffed the winds of trade and decided that Hanigan was a man he might well do business with. Knowing that Hanigan might be persuaded to put up the site for sale, Donald Trump got to work. As usual, he started out doing his homework, making a preliminary study of Genesco, Inc.

It was a revealing one. Genesco had an interesting number of big store chains—important ones. Bonwit Teller, Tiffany, Henri Bendel, among others.

As for the best site in New York . . .

Genesco owned Bonwit Teller, but, ironically, *not* the land on which it was built. It was the land that Donald lusted after. Not the store. And guess who owned the land? Lady Luck must certainly have been hiding her smile as she watched Donald Trump search out the truth. The Equitable Life Assurance Society owned the site.

Equitable was happy with Donald Trump. It would in all certainty smile on his proposals. Probably. And so in his mind, Donald was already creating a new project. This would involve another partnership, just as his deal with Hyatt had involved a partnership. In this situation, Equitable would put up the land, and Donald would put up the building.

What Donald proposed from the first was to repeat the Grand Hyatt job. In other words, he would gut the building, level it, and build his own—on land owned by Equitable.

The critical point in Trump's proposal involved yet another aspect of the deal. He wanted to build a fantastic, dramatic structure right in the middle of Fifth Avenue, the most posh and stable of New York's shopping streets. And therein lay the worm in the bud.

The zoning laws were such that he would be allowed only to put up a modest-sized building on the same square footage occupied by Bonwit Teller's current building.

But there were ways to get around the rigid zoning laws. On

the same block with Bonwit Teller's stood Tiffany's. It was never in Donald Trump's mind to buy Tiffany's and tear it down to give him more land area. He wanted that most prestigious of stores next door to his proposed building. But by keeping Tiffany's adjacent to his building, he would be sacrificing a certain amount of the dramatic flair he envisioned in a very tall, dominant structure.

But there were air rights to consider.

Air rights?

In the crazy Byzantine world of the city's building codes, a building's height and girth (measure of circumference) was limited to a specific formula—a magic formula called the Floor Area Ratio (FAR). Briefly, that meant that the total square footage of a building could be no more than a specific multiple of the square footage of the building lot. Again, there were arcane ways in which to get what were called "bonuses" that would extend the total square footage of the building area, but they were tricky.

The Bonwit Teller lot had an absolute maximum FAR of 21.6. At Der Scutt's first computations, the architect found that the maximum height for Donald's building would be a twenty-story structure with ten thousand square feet of usable space per floor. The same area, however, could be computed as a forty-story building with five thousand square feet of space per floor.

One of the bonuses mentioned above was an item called air rights. At first glance, air rights would seem to mean the use of the air space above a building—that is, a cantilevered approach of an adjacent building. Generally speaking, however, air rights are simply part of the maddening mumbo-jumbo of zoning laws in general.

Air rights could be computed into the FAR formula of one building to take advantage of an adjoining building's square footage area. That is, building A could purchase the so-called air rights of building B, and add building B's square footage of lot area to the original square footage of building A.

So, if Donald could buy Tiffany's air rights, he could include a portion of Tiffany's square footage area to compute the size of his planned structure.

Tiffany's was not going to change. Not if Donald Trump could help it. He knew that if he could purchase Tiffany's air rights, he could erect a building of much more dramatic impact.

His next move was to meet with Walter Hoving, who at that time still owned Tiffany's. Hoving met with him and agreed to sell the air rights to Tiffany's.

Now that the fundamentals of the deal had been struck, Donald and Ivana began working with Der Scutt on the design of the building Trump was going to erect. Although Ivana knew little about architecture per se—her father was an electrical engineer, not an architectural designer—she was familiar with blueprints and all the paraphernalia of construction. And she had apparently inherited some of her father's engineering talents one way or another.

One of the primary reasons for the success of the Grand Hyatt on Forty-second Street was its incredibly striking lobby—created by what designers call the atrium effect. Atrium is a Latin word that refers to the main open room of a Roman house; actually, it is an open courtyard around which a Roman or Greek house is built. In New York City, of course, the atrium usually becomes a closed-over open space, to effect a kind of wide-openness within a closed space.

What is especially interesting about New York's zoning laws was that the use of the atrium concept became a bonus that could be used in the FAR formula. Thus, by utilizing an atrium as he had in the design of the Grand Hyatt, Donald could get an even bigger building above it.

It was Ivana who approached the design with a brand-new concept in shopping. It was her opinion that by using the atrium concept in the entrance to the new building, there would be room for several floors of small and exclusive shops built to fit right into the lobby itself as part of its decor.

Ivana was not quite as insular as most typical New Yorkers. For some years now the mall concept had swept the country—in effect the typical shopping mall is a huge atrium glassed over at the top to keep out the elements—but the idea had not yet seemed to reach and penetrate the consciousness of New York City. Ivana had seen malls in Toronto and in Montreal; she knew they worked.

This would be an elaboration of the mall concept as the entryway to the building. Although Der Scutt worked it out in quite an exciting way, Donald was not really sure the atrium would act as a stimulant to sales. But of course, now that he had become a believer in her instincts, he went along with Ivana's idea.

"Even if the atrium wasn't terribly successful," Donald wrote, "the bonus I'd get for building it—several extra floors in my residential tower—would more than make up for its cost."

Daring Donald. Cautious Donald. He believed, but he did not believe. Like many daring people, he was always consciously and successfully covering his backside.

And so . . .

They might be taking a chance. Shoppers might not like to go into a strange open space inside a building to visit small shops. And floor space would have to be limited. And ground floor space in any store was always the most profitable.

But it was time to take a shot at it.

Another important element in the design where Ivana had enough input to be mentioned in Donald's autobiography was in the overall shape and profile of the building itself. Der Scutt had tried all sorts of designs to get the proper dramatic effect, but nothing seemed to work. Every profile looked inadequate.

Finally, working together, they came up with a system of terraces stepped back from the street to the height of the Tiffany building next door. From there on, the tower went up with a sawtooth design at the top. This gave a zig-zag effect, and the building wound up having twenty-eight different sides. Facets, they were called.

By now the three designers were calling it Trump Tower. And Trump Tower it became. From the beginning, Donald said that Trump Tower would have the "finest apartments in the top building in the best location in the world."

Ivana pledged herself to see that his intentions were carried out to the last detail. With the Grand Hyatt finally running at a profit, there was no need for her to supervise it any longer. Now, to the relief of the people operating the Grand Hyatt, she spent all her time in the selection of wallpaper, curtains, and other details of interior decoration for the apartments in Trump Tower.

Most important was the decor and appearance of the atrium, which Ivana secretly thought would be the centerpiece of the whole building—just as the lobby of the Grand Hyatt is. To find exactly the proper shade of marble, she flew to Italy to track it down.

In the end, she selected a type of marble called *breccia pernice*. The word *breccia* means "a type of rock consisting of sharp fragments embedded in a fine-grained matrix (sand or clay)." The word *pernice* is Italian for partridge—the word used to describe the texture and striped appearance of the rock.

In appearance, it was a weird blend of pink, rose, and peach tones. Because it was rare, it was incredibly expensive—even within the parameters of Donald Trump's resources. When Ivana Trump went to the quarry to supervise the selection of each individual rock, she discovered that much of the visible material contained large white spots and white veins that took away from the dramatic effect of the pinks and roses that were her primary reason for choosing the marble. Many of the surfaces seemed diseased to her.

"That was jarring to me and took away from the beauty of the stone," Donald Trump said later. He wanted to forget it and get something else that would be easier to quarry.

But Ivana was determined to have this special rock face and argued with him for some time about it. He finally bowed to her wishes. But he insisted that Ivana go to the quarry and mark off the slabs that were to be used.

She tramped the quarry from one end to the other and marked off all the good slabs with strips of black tape. The rest of the marble—about two-thirds of it—was simply scrapped. There were 250 tons of marble quarried for Trump Tower.

Ivana even mentioned once that Trump Tower cost Italy the whole top of a mountain.

Once shipped to the building site, Ivana supervised the cutting and laying of the marble, along with her husband. In her meticulous no-nonsense way, she made sure that every piece was shaped exactly right, and in turn, that it was perfectly matched and laid properly to the adjacent piece. She knew that all the designs and the symmetry of the rock had to be right, or the effect would be totally ruined.

On one of her routine inspections, she noticed that there was a hairline crack in one of the stone faces. Apparently it had occurred after setting. She summoned her husband and the two of them made the work crew remove the slab and put in a new one while they watched.

This did not endear Ivana to the workmen—some of whom

may have worked with her at the Grand Hyatt. As for those who did not know her, they said what they thought about her, and she ignored any remarks they made.

"What is important?" she said. "My feelings? Or the perfection of Trump Tower?"

In the end, the color of the marble in the atrium turned out to be one of the main features of the building—a memorable impression that all people entering and looking about carry away with them.

She was criticized for marblizing in hot pink rather than a more traditional color. She simply shrugged. "What do they prefer?" she asked rhetorically, referring to anyone who disagreed with her. "The cheap white travertine that is used in banks? It is too cold, too common. Donald and I are more daring than that."

Indeed, the colorful *breccia pernice* was used not only in the atrium, but was laid at least six floors up past the atrium on all the corridor walls. This gives the surroundings a very opulent feel—the kind of thing, as Ivana had known from the start, that would make visitors want to luxuriate in the feeling of splendor and open up their pocketbooks to spend a little money.

Ivana indulged herself in the open-air space that was generated in the atrium, as much as she had indulged herself in the expansive feeling generated by the Grand Hyatt lobby. It was her recommendation at Trump Tower that the railings in the atrium be made of polished brass rather than the cheaper more manageable aluminum. Of course, the brass was a great deal more expensive—not only to buy but to maintain—and yet it adds to the feeling of voluptuousness in the atrium.

Also, the brass blends in perfectly with the exotic color of the marble.

In addition, Ivana was instrumental in suggesting the use of reflective glass to make the rather small space allocated to the atrium look even bigger.

But the main element that really makes the atrium work is one of Ivana's most precious dreams: the waterfall.

Originally, it had been decided that the four walls of the atrium would be hung with huge dramatic paintings or other art forms of a conventional nature. Then some thought was expended on creating a sculptured wall on the eastern side—the back wall—of the atrium. It was Ivana who began fighting for the waterfall that was eventually adopted. To her, paintings were simply too old-fashioned and strait-laced to suffice in this exceptional environment. What she wanted was an even bigger and more dramatic and more sweeping entryway than the lobby of the Grand Hyatt.

She had, of course, helped design the waterfall in the Grand Hyatt. In fact, it was her insistence on getting it to stop burbling and bubbling that made it into the muted masterpiece it has become. This one, she vowed, would outdo the other.

Indeed it does. The waterfall in the Trump Tower atrium eventually turned out to be nearly eighty feet high. Using the same expertise she had on the Grand Hyatt waterfall, Ivana worked with the construction crew from the beginning, not giving up until she was satisfied that they had gotten it right.

But Ivana's influence was not confined to the atrium, although it is most evident there. Her work extended to the residential units that started at the thirtieth floor and went on up to the top of the building. Nevertheless, a great deal less attention was paid to the interior work on these apartments than on the atrium at the bottom of the structure.

Ivana knew that anyone who would be able to spend a million dollars for a two-bedroom apartment in Trump Tower, or five million on a four-bedroom duplex, was going to get his own designer, rip out the interior of the extant apartment, and rebuild it to fit his or her own tastes.

Most of the residential apartments were higher than the surrounding buildings, and commanded sensational views to the north all the way to Central Park, to the south to the Statue of Liberty, to the east to the East River, and to the west to the Hudson River. Most apartments had views in at least two directions. The windows were designed almost from floor to ceiling.

Still, perfection was always in Ivana's mind—regardless of expense. One day she noticed that there was a narrow gap between the trim on the wall and the wall of an elevator. If the trim were changed, which was the obvious thing a carpenter would suggest, it would be visible because the trim on the opposite side would not match it in width. Rather than do such a patchwork job, Ivana ordered the entire car removed, to be replaced with another built to the proper specifications.

The story made the rounds and became something of a cause

célèbre in the history of the building. But then, Ivana was always creating legends.

So indeed was The Donald. Der Scutt once told the story of what happened in Donald's conference room when construction on Trump Tower fell fifteen days behind schedule. Donald was furious. "I don't think anything scares me," he once said. "My general attitude is to attack life."

In the instance of the fifteen-day delay, he attacked elsewhere. He was so beside himself with rage that he kicked a chair all the way across the conference room where he was working with his associates.

"He ruined a new pair of Gucci loafers," Scutt recalled. "He always has to have his way."

Ivana also helped Donald with the details of the landscaping of the atrium. This was a particularly sensitive issue with the two of them. Because the landscaping—live shrubs, flowers, and trees—proved so successful at the Grand Hyatt, the Trumps were determined to spare no expense in making the Trump Tower atrium perfect.

Every day the landscaping was checked to make sure that everything was just so. It cost a small fortune to truck an entire forest of forty-foot-high trees from Florida to New York. It was cold weather when the trees were finally brought into the city. In order to protect them from the frost, the Trumps had a tunnel dug beneath the building to house the trees temporarily.

When they were finally installed on a lower garden level, Ivana took one look at them and decided that they were too large and would dominate the lobby in a way that would decrease its effectiveness. In fact, the trees became the centerpiece of the atrium, rather than all the other elements Ivana had been at such pains to keep in proper balance. She told the workers the trees must go. Now! Immediately!

Donald arrived during this contretemps. He took one look at the forest of green and had to agree with Ivana. But by now there was absolutely no way to get the trees out of the atrium intact. Besides, they would probably die in the frigid weather outside. Even to remove them one by one would undoubtedly cause a great amount of destruction—scratches on the highly polished marble surfaces, gouges in the polished flooring, breakage of glass, and so on—and so it was decided that a crew of workmen would come in with chain saws and cut them all down.

And it was done exactly that way.

Ivana and Donald were also concerned with a huge screen of hanging ivy that trailed down from the wall at the upper part of the atrium. For some reason, no matter how much it was trimmed and tended to, it developed a ragged look that anyone who has grown ivy will understand.

Because Ivana did not know how to handle the vines, she suggested that they approach Helen Murphy, who was going to open a flower shop in the lobby of Trump Tower. Murphy managed to get the ivy in shape, after which she was hired to complete the difficult landscaping of the atrium.

Trump Tower was opened for occupancy in 1982. The atrium was still under construction, but finally opened in April. Paul Goldberger reviewed the opening for *The New York Times*. According to him, the atrium at Trump Tower was "turning out to be a much more pleasant addition to the cityscape than the architectural oddsmakers would have had it." The story went on to say that the atrium might well be "the most pleasant interior public space to be completed in New York in some years. It is warm, luxurious and even exhilarating—in every way more welcoming than the public arcades and atriums that have preceded it in buildings like Olympic Tower, the Galleria, and Citicorp Center."

At the time of its opening there were 263 condominiums on the upper levels of the the building, ranging in price from eight hundred thousand to ten million. Of these, eighty-five percent were sold. The owners were such superstars as Johnny Carson, Stephen Spielberg, Sophia Loren, Paul Anka, David Merrick, and the late Liberace.

Interestingly enough, the building is actually fifty-eight stories in height. Nevertheless the public sees it as sixty-eight stories in height. This effect was achieved through a bit of creative floor numbering on the part of the Trumps.

For example, what was called the thirtieth floor—the first residential floor—was actually the twentieth floor, counting from the bottom. The Trumps claimed that they were justified in making the first residential floor the thirtieth rather than the twentieth because of the height of five stories of retail space in the atrium, which only counted as one floor in reality. Where the other five floors came from—or went to—was never clearly established.

It was the *Wall Street Journal* that pointed out the fact that the Trumps had used a great deal of creative numbering at the Grand Hyatt, as well as at Trump Tower. The first floor of guest rooms at the Grand Hyatt, actually six stories up, is numbered the fourteenth floor in the hotel. Oh well, who counts floors anyway? Many buildings in New York and other cities have no thirteenth floor at all—by number, anyway—as a kind of tip of the hat to centuries of superstition. Perhaps it's best not to be too particular; just push the elevator button and ride up without worrying.

Donald Trump's detractors call all this playing around with numbers a form of hype, and label it deceptive. The Trumps have never issued any kind of statement on the subject—either in defense or in explanation.

Trump Tower is a dazzling display of kitsche and glitz. Certain New Yorkers burdened with more traditional taste do not like the flashy gold trim around the entrance. In addition, the name TRUMP, which was set off in the facade in two-foot-high bronze letters, puts them off entirely.

Even Der Scutt has a word to say about that. "I tried to tell Donald about the value of understatement, like the small lettering on Tiffany's next door, but he wouldn't listen."

There are those however, who come in from the outside—tourists, out-of-towners, suburbanites—and love the look and feel of the building. One of the most spectacular details are the uniforms in which the doormen are dressed.

These were designed by Ivana. Jerome Tuccille described them as "ornamental costumes that made them resemble somewhat South American generals on dress-parade. They wore dark blue trousers with gold piping down the sides and outsized hats that nearly hid their faces."

Ivana contracted to have these costumes made in London, to bring, as she said, a "touch of Buckingham Palace" to the doormen at Trump Tower. She was somewhat perturbed by the barbs of criticism aimed at these designs. "They are fun," she said. "Why must everyone be so serious?" And she did indeed have a point. What was wrong with looking at fashion as just a bit amusing?

It is the striking pink marble floors and walls of Trump Tower that catches everybody's eye. The glass, the chrome, the waterfall, the ivy, the handrails, the brass—they are all part of the effect.

And in the midst of all this glittering display sits a man in black-tie and tails at a gleaming grand piano, playing tinkling melodies from Broadway hits of years gone by.

"It's become a happening!" Donald Trump exulted. "It's a great tourist place. People love it. We're one hundred percent rented. There are lots of people here, the right kind of people."

Now that Trump Tower was open and was a success, Ivana could turn her attention to another area of her life. She was pregnant once again and had been during much of the excitement of preparing Trump Tower for its opening.

But the Trumps were into another project now, and Ivana was still Executive Vice President in charge of Interior Design for the Trump Organization.

Donald's third building project in New York City was the construction of Trump Plaza—a residential building on Third Avenue. It was costing $125 million, and was supposed to open in February 1984.

Every morning Ivana would travel across town to check up on the construction crew and see that The Donald's orders were being carried out.

As usual, the construction schedule was tight, and Ivana knew she had to make sure everyone was toeing the mark. With her characteristic meticulous attention to detail, she was supervising every aspect of the building's decoration.

One morning as she arrived, Ivana spotted a flash of bright yellow on one of the balconies that was cantilevered out over the sidewalk on Third Avenue. Immediately, she went into a flurry of action. She rushed for the nearest telephone. The work crew had rigged up a temporary phone in the incompleted lobby, and it was from there she reached her husband.

He was not long in arriving at the construction site.

"What's wrong?" he asked her.

She pointed up to one of the balconies where the handrail could be easily seen.

"It's yellow. Yellow isn't right."

After a consultation, Donald called the head of the construction company doing the job, and soon he, too, was on the site. Irving

Fischer arrived in a cab, and before he even got out and paid the driver, The Donald was on him.

"The color! It's yellow, flat yellow, like a—"

Fischer remembered him looking down the street, and spotting the color he wanted.

"See that gold Cadillac down the street? That's the color I want those handrails. Gold. Cadillac Gold. Not yellow like a daisy."

Fischer related that he had to go out and buy "goddamned Cadillac paint for the railings."

The new color suited Ivana. And things settled down at Trump Plaza.

Meanwhile, Ivana and Donald were discussing the future. They needed a bigger place to live—why not make a slight change in their place of residence? Donald Trump had reserved a $10 million triplex penthouse in Trump Tower for himself, but had not yet sat down to figure out how best to utilize the space for his family.

Ivana and Donald went out one night and visited billionaire Adnan Khashoggi's apartment in nearby Olympic Tower. Both Trumps were awed by its size—"approximately the size of a Persian Gulf sheikdom," *Time* magazine noted.

And so Donald moved. He studied his own triplex, decided it was much too dinky, and added to it an adjoining and unsold triplex, and then started to do what he had always enjoyed doing best.

He ripped it all apart and hauled away all the original walls and floors. And then he started all over again.

What resulted is a fifty-room, $10 million apartment that takes up the top three floors of Trump Tower. He and Ivana were fascinated with onyx. The Trumps's living quarters at Trump Tower features onyx liberally—onyx baseboards run along all the walls; their bathtub is made of lilac onyx. The tub operates with gold-plated faucets, of course.

"Onyx is like a precious jewel," Donald said, "many grades above marble."

But it is the living room that is the jewel in the crown. It is eighty feet in length. It has bronze-edged floor-to-ceiling windows that overlook Central Park. And—the climax of the entire remodeling extravaganza—a twelve-foot waterfall set against a backdrop of translucent onyx right there in the living room!

There are hand-carved marble columns, and walls lined in Italian gold onyx, and ceiling moldings in twenty-three-carat gold.

"There has never been anything like this built in four hundred years," Trump told *Time* magazine. "He is thinking of the Vatican," *Time* noted, "ignoring, say, the Palace of Versailles."

In 1989 the Trumps moved into their new penthouse apartment.

"Sometimes when I look at Trump Tower," Ivana said, "and I think of its impact and success, I realize it hasn't really hit me that we *own* it!"

Chapter Eight
Living It Up

The weekend house at Wainscott, Long Island, had in many ways become unsatisfactory to the life style that was now opening up to Ivana Trump. At first it was perfect for a pair of newlyweds, and Ivana remembered with nostalgia those marvelous afternoons at the Maidstone Country Club when she and Donald would meet for lunch and then spend an afternoon playing tennis. It was a life that was low-keyed and languorous, and perfect for newlyweds.

For their uncluttered life at the time, it had been the perfect place to relax far from the Manhattan crowd. But as soon as Donald, Jr. left babyhood, the rather informal atmosphere of the place wore a bit thin—at least on Ivana's patience.

The Trumps needed room to breathe on their weekends. What Ivana decided she wanted was a great deal more space. She wanted a real retreat where the family could weekend, away from the hustle and bustle of the city—not too far, but not too near.

Also, she thought peace and quiet would help both Donald and her relax. She always liked the idea of spending therapy time on weekends—a spot of quality time for her to do a bit of gardening. Perhaps if she looked around she could find a place more conducive to the sedate country life style that a weekend gardener needed.

There was a story, which gained currency in early profiles of Ivana Trump, that she persuaded The Donald to rent her a helicopter, supply her with a pilot, and send her up in the skies to look down on and find a suitable spot for their weekend home. Apocryphal or not, it was true that Donald might well have selected that means to appease his wife's insistence on a property search.

Several general areas were put up for investigation. The Trumps had visited Donald's lawyer, Roy Cohn, many times at his weekend retreat in the heavily wooded part of Greenwich, Connecticut, just over the border from New York. The Trumps both approved of the area, but were a bit reluctant to adopt Cohn's love of absolute silence, isolation, and infinite distance from other people.

And so the idea of a woodland retreat was out. Both Ivana and Donald liked swimming. While not at all what might be considered a yachtsman, Donald may have always had a dream of sometime owning a craft and piloting it wherever his whimsy took him.

Donald, Jr. was old enough to enjoy the beach. That was a primary consideration. The shore seemed the place to locate rather than inland. Noise and energy have a way of dissipating themselves along the sea and shore.

The Trumps began to explore the area around Greenwich, Connecticut—whether on the ground or from the air is moot—and finally settled on an area of private beachs owned by a group of owners of impressive structures built overlooking the water.

The mansion Ivana and Donald found was located on one of the inlets along the lower Connecticut coast called Indian Harbor. Indian Harbor is a protected cove located between two fingers of land jutting out into Long Island Sound. Through traffic—read, outsiders, that is, people like you and me—is prohibited on the winding roads that connect the mansions built there.

These access roadways have names like Oneida Court, Orchard Wood, Chimney Corner Lane, and Indian Chase Drive. Physically, the area is roughly a mile from the Greenwich railroad station, but psychically, it is light years away. It is set off from the world of ordinary human beings by a guard post.

In his book on Donald Trump, Jerome Tuccille noted that in style and appearance the house they bought in Greenwich was a lookalike for the type of house that Fred Trump erected in Jamaica Estates for the well-heeled during the early decades of this century. In fact, the house in Greenwich was built in 1939.

It is Georgian in appearance—Georgian because of the red-brick facade and the wide white shutters—even though it is not Georgian at all in feeling. Georgian houses were town houses, built in long rows on English or Irish city streets; squared off; curbside fronted; attached. This mansion is low—only two-storied—and rambles over a large area of ground at the top of a sloping hill.

At first glance, one would assume that it was the kind of hotel one might have registered in at the turn of the century at a favorite resort such as Saratoga Springs. It would be easy to imagine the ghost of Ingrid Bergman fanning herself under a large umbrella in the sun.

The main part of the house is approached from the side by a wide promenade, with two huge doors protected by porticos in the center. The central portion then slopes up—in typical Cape Cod fashion—to a high clock tower rising above the entrance.

The rest of the house extends out into a long wing that continues and continues. In the rear of the house stands a glassed-in flagstone porch that faces the water. The main entrance of the mansion is approached by a short rise of circular stone steps that winds between two high stone columns. At each side of this walk there are bushes and shrubbery that is always well tended. The front door is protected by a portico composed of four white columns, supporting a captain's walk above the entryway.

The view from the porch at the rear is absolutely spectacular. A rolling lawn stretches away, down and down and down, to Long Island Sound. There the property ends in an abrupt sand pit.

In all, the estate covers about five acres.

The interior decor was every bit as pretentious, but as real, as the exterior. It was simply ostentation from another era, and even though peculiar, as straightforward as that earlier ostentation had been. The house was built at the height of the Great Depression—and so might well have been some developer's idea of trying to rekindle the dream of wealth and opulence in some lucky millionaire who escaped the market crash and might want to show off his luck.

There are parking spots for at least seven automobiles in the garages. There are dozens of bedrooms, dining rooms, living rooms, bathrooms, pantries, family rooms, rumpus rooms, and a huge kitchen. There are rooms for the servants; there are separate apartments for the caretaker and the superintendant of the grounds.

But what particularly excited Ivana was the fact that there is a separate greenhouse for her gardening activities. And, of course, there is a dock down at the edge of the lawn where it reaches the Sound.

Upon examination, the Trumps found that the place was for sale at an asking price of $5.2 million. Of all the places they had looked at, this one seemed to them to be the best. There was a very real sense of isolation here. The quiet and the calm seemed to settle over them when they drove through the barricades and approached the house.

For Ivana it was a definite yes. For Donald it was—well, let's wait and see.

Donald was figuring he could get the sellers down below the $5.2 million mark. There were few enough people who had the millions to spend on a property like that. It was said to have been originally the home of the family that had made a fortune in the manufacture of crayons.

Trump-like, Donald began to get to work on the real estate agents. He pointed out flaws, problems. He showed them how impossible the place was to sell. He kept at them as only Donald Trump could keep at people.

In the end, the Trumps bought the place for $3.7 million—a million and a half dollars below the asking price!

They signed the papers in 1982.

But of course before moving in, the place had to be touched up. Ivana and Donald went over every inch of the property. By now Ivana was getting into the swing of checking out the details. If she could make the Grand Hyatt into the showplace it was as Executive Vice President in charge of Design, she could certainly make her own home look right!

And so, quite soon, painters, carpenters, electricians, plumbers, and various other craftsmen were swarming all over renovating the mansion.

One of these workers was a Greenwich artist named Ann George. She was hired to refurbish a ceiling mural in the main house—to spruce it up, and to snap up its colors. Jerome Tuccille interviewed her for his book on Trump.

"When I finished the ceiling mural," Ann told him, Donald said that "he liked it very much but there was one thing he wanted me to change. His eye picked out the one thing in the whole painting that I would have changed myself, but was hoping no one would notice. He zeroed right in on it."

According to Tuccille, the artist felt that Donald was a very tough boss, but she admitted that he knew how to get the best work out of people. "I can't believe how much I put into that ceiling. I'm amazed when I see what I've done. But that's one of his talents. He gets the best out of you, always pushing you to reach your full potential."

As for Ivana, the artist saw her as a very warm and down-to-earth person—a very good person. "She likes having all the money, but she's not affectatious about it. She appreciates the art, the painting, all the fine things the money can bring her. But she's not driven by it."

The acquisition of the Greenwich mansion and the birth of Ivana's second child occurred in the same year. The two events coincided, and reinforced the impression in the public's mind that the Trumps were starting to form some kind of royal—or at least democratic—dynasty. The second child, incidentally, was a girl; named somewhat exotically but appropriately, Ivanka.

Now, with their weekend home ready for habitation, perhaps the family would expand even further!

The retreat turned out to be perfect for the growing Trump family. Sometimes Ivana would come up on Friday, and stay through Monday. It all depended on what was going on in the city.

"I think the quality of living in Greenwich is just special," Ivana told a reporter from the *Greenwich Time.* "The people, they mind their own business. As much as we can be free, the Trumps can be free in Greenwich."

Ivana went on expounding on the very special life she had there. "When we come to our country home, we really want to be together as a family. We don't want to go to parties. In Greenwich there is not a big social life. Well, maybe there is, but I don't know about it.

"I want, let's say, to put on the pants and the T-shirt and the gloves, and go and dig in the garden. We like to go to the movie theaters, and, here, people don't approach you. They're distinguished enough already so that they just leave you alone."

Let's now look at how Greenwich affected Donald, the man who never even stood still without trying to exert his influence on everything around him—particularly things dealing in any way with real estate.

In the summer of 1985, three years after the purchase of the Greenwich estate, Donald Trump applied to the directors of Indian Harbor Properties—from whom he had purchased the immense retreat—for permission to subdivide his land and sell off parts of it as building lots. What he apparently wanted was to break up the five acres of undeveloped land and develop them himself. And, given Donald's history, who should have been surprised about that?

Surprised or not, the uptight Indian Harbor inhabitants immediately rejected his application out of hand.

About the same time, Donald caused a flurry of excitement when he approached a Greenwich man named Joe Keating, who owned a motel and restaurant called the Showboat Inn just down the road from the Railroad Station. Donald wanted to purchase the motel and restaurant to refurbish it.

Translation: Gut it? Flatten it? Build Trump Inn?

Probably.

Keating was appalled at the idea, according to his Greenwich neighbors. Further investigation tended to bear out the theory that Ivana and Donald had become concerned about the noise of the weekend yachtsmen who used the showboat's marina. If Donald could buy it, he could probably dispose of the racket simply by closing it and holding it as a piece of undeveloped property.

The Showboat was, in Keating's words, not for sale.

Ironically, in late 1989 word went out in the local newspapers that the Showboat Inn was having a rough time financially, and was up for bidding by auction. (No further words on this as this book goes to press.)

Indian Harbor Properties never gave Ivana and Donald permission to subdivide; chances are that the group never will.

Both Ivana and Donald continued to keep a wary eye out for good real estate properties, and at the same time they were searching for and found the Greenwich mansion, they located another prospect that was even more spectacular; but was far removed from the New York metropolitan area. It was called Mar-a-Lago—Spanish for Sea-to-Lake—in Palm Beach, Florida. The mansion stretched from the shores of the Atlantic Ocean to Lake Worth on the eighteen acres of land.

Unlike the mansion in Greenwich, this house had a glamorous story attached to it. Built by Marjorie Merriweather Post in 1923, it had often been considered a monument to the ostentation of the roaring twenties.

Post was one of the more memorable heiresses of that era. She attracted and married a number of very rich men, including E.

F. Hutton. Yes, indeed, the same one the television commercials used to cite with the memorable voice-over that went "When E. F. Hutton speaks, people listen."

In fact, Barbara Hutton was Marjorie Post's cousin. Marjorie's daughter, Nedenia Hutton, changed her name to Dina Merrill when she became an actress and was later the wife of actor Cliff Robertson.

Marjorie Post was also married to Joseph Davies, President Franklin D. Roosevelt's Ambassador to Russia; as such she was one of the first American women to represent America to the Russians. Post was married and divorced four times; and she was "one of the most aggressive hostesses who ever lived," according to her biographer William Wright.

Marjorie Post's own money came from breakfast food. Her father was Charles William Post, who invented a popular substitute for coffee in the late nineteenth century which he called Postum—an act of self-promotion that would put him well within the milieu of a much later self-promoter named Donald John Trump.

Postum was an instant success, and C. W. Post followed it up in 1898 with another sure-fire product—nutty little crunchies he called Grape-Nuts. They didn't taste at all like grapes. Actually, C. W. used the term for grape-shot (tiny pellets used in battle) to describe the shape, and nuts to describe the flavor. The dry cereal was an instant success.

But C. W. wasn't through yet. He noticed an interesting concoction developed by one of the Kellogg brothers. The Kelloggs were Dr. John Harvey Kellogg and W. K. Kellogg. It was Dr. John Harvey who invented a flaking operation by which he could cook corn or wheat pulp on large drums and then flake it off. But he never bothered to market it as a product.

C. W. did, as had other entrepreneurs before him. It appeared in 1906. But he was not satisfied with the name. He had first tried Elijah's Manna, but the Bible-thumpers were outraged. It was sacrilegious. Again, acting on instinct the way Donald Trump would decades later, he came up with the self-promoting name Post-Toasties. He was well on his way to a fortune. His product worked, while those of his competitors did not.

Marjorie Merriweather Post's celebrity was as a hostess, not as a wife or even a mistress. All her parties were covered by the media of the day, even by stringers for the solid and dignified *New York Times*. It was impossible to pass them up, especially when people like the Duke and Duchess of Windsor seemed to constantly arrive to be courted and charmed by the local citizens.

She used to give evening square dance parties. If you were invited, you knew you were in. If you weren't invited, you simply lay back in a hot tub and opened your veins.

In spite of all the excitement, Post lived at Mar-a-Lago only two months of the year, between Christmas and Washington's Birthday, which used to be celebrated on February 22. On that date, Palm Beach always had an official Birthday Ball in honor of our first president.

For fifty years Post reigned as the social lionness of Palm Beach. Finally, in 1963, she tired of it all, and offered the estate to the state of Florida for use as an educational seminar site and a meeting place for high-level government officials.

State officials, turning pale at the thought of the $200,000 yearly maintenance bill, refused her generous offer. In 1973 Post died, and her family then gave Mar-a-Lago to the United States Department of the Interior as a retreat for presidents and heads of state.

In 1980, however, the U.S. government returned the estate to the Post Foundation; by that time the annual cost of its maintenance had zoomed up to a cool one million per year. The Post Foundation was nervously trying to keep the mansion in repair when Ivana and Donald saw it in 1982.

The Trumps then put in a bid of fifteen million dollars for the Post mansion. The government was asking for twenty-five million. And so the government turned down the Trump's bid, and continued to search for another buyer.

Several other bidders put in offers, all at higher prices than that offered by the Trumps. These offers were all subsequently processed by the government, but in each case, the negotiations eventually broke down.

Mostly the problems dealt with what the potential purchasers wanted to do with the property. Several wanted to subdivide the land and change it in many different ways. These buyers included a Houston developer and the Marriott Corporation. Others wanted to change the property into an entertainment center, a hotel, or whatever. Many of the problems involved financing in general.

As these deals all fell through, one by one, Ivana and Donald would immediately counter bid, but at a lower figure than the time before. And they were turned down each time.

Late in 1985, Ivana and Donald changed their bid offer in one specific detail. They made it a cash offer of five million dollars, plus another three million in cash for the furnishings, as they stood, in the house. Even though it was a much lower offer than their previous bids, it was one that, apparently, could not be refused.

By now the Department of the Interior was fed up with trying to get rid of this white elephant. The broken deals and withdrawn offers had wasted taxpayer's money for months and simply gotten nowhere. Quite suddenly, the government accepted the Trumps's offer.

A month later the papers were signed and the house was theirs. The local paper ran a front-page story about the "bargain-basement" price at which the Post property had been sold. The headline read:

MAR-A-LAGO'S BARGAIN PRICE ROCKS COMMUNITY

The Post mansion had taken four years to build in the 1920s. When finished, it contained 118 rooms, although some descriptions of the mansion mention only 110 and others mention 130.

Details of the construction staggered the local citizenry and tended to bear out accusations of ostentation and conspicuous consumption.

For example, its construction required that three boatloads of dorian stone, quarried in Italy, be sailed across the Atlantic to provide material for the exterior walls.

From Spain the builders purchased thirty-six thousand roof tiles that dated back to the fifteenth century; these were used both on the exterior and in the interior of the house.

Almost everyone who has ever seen the mansion is in agreement that no matter how many rooms it has it is still one of the world's most spectacular single-family residences in existence.

It was, according to the Trumps, "one of the greatest properties in the United States. . . . It is one of the diamonds of real estate. . . . It is in a class by itself. To me, Marjorie Merriweather Post is one of the truly fascinating ladies of an era. She had a kind of style that is unique. She was highly intelligent and extremely gracious." As for why the Trumps decided to buy the mansion, Donald said, "I think every bit of [the aura she gave it] should be preserved."

Ivana and Donald learned one important public-relations lesson in their Greenwich adventure. Donald did not talk about dismantling Mar-a-Lago, unlike his offer to buy the Showboat Inn, only to rip it down and build a new one.

The Trumps announced, instead, that there would definitely be no changes made in the house. And this announcement delighted the people of Palm Beach. "I want to make sure I don't disturb its special quality," Donald said. "I want to make sure I keep it in a shape we can all be proud of."

And, fittingly, once the papers were signed, Donald Trump officially presented the entire estate as a gift to Ivana Trump, making her the mistress of Mar-a-Lago. Shortly thereafter, Ivana Trump hired a Palm Beach interior designer to refurbish the huge mansion.

Buffy Donlon had restored a number of houses and buildings in the Southeast. Ivana had seen and been impressed with some of them and selected her to do the job on the Post mansion. Donlon was born Doris Beverly Davis, the daughter of Fred Davis, a professional athlete who played tackle for the Chicago Bears football team during the 1940s.

Donlon graduated from the University of Alabama, and began to ply her decorating trade by designing office buildings, restaurants, hospitals, and yachts—as well as luxury homes for clients in posh resort areas like Hilton Head, South Carolina. In 1978 she formed an interior decorating firm called Foxhill, named after a home in which she had lived in Selma, Alabama.

Donlon was immediately struck with Ivana's talents and expertise. "She has beautiful taste," she said. "She knows what she's doing."

But there was more to Donlon's appreciation of Ivana than simply her taste. "It's wonderful to work in an atmosphere in which the owners want to do the right thing for Mar-a-Lago," she said. "They want to keep the house in tune with what Mrs. Post wanted when she built the house. We're not going to redecorate the house; rather we are refurbishing, bringing it back to its original beauty."

The mansion simply has to be seen to be believed. It was designed by a Viennese immigrant named Joseph Urban, who claimed that he had designed buildings for Emperor Franz Joseph in Austria before coming to America. None of his credentials were ever found.

What Urban actually did was work on Broadway. In the first years of her marriage to Edward F. Hutton, Marjorie was friendly with Florenz Ziegfeld, the famous Broadway producer, and his wife, Billie Burke. Through them, Marjorie Post met Joseph Urban, who was working in the theater as a set designer for the Ziegfield Follies.

And so it was Urban who dreamed up what became Mar-a-Lago. He had the help, however, of an imaginative sketch artist named Ju-Ju du Blas, who constantly tossed off visual concepts of wildly impossible chambers and corridors to be utilized in the finished interior of the mansion.

Eventually a third architect, Marion Sims Wyeth, was added to help Urban with the more technical—read, engineering—aspects of the mansion's working drawings. The actual construction began in 1923. At first the mansion seemed to be part Spanish, part Moorish, part Arabian Nights fantasy, with just a little bit of Italian thrown in to make for a completely eclectic mix.

For example, there were tapestries of all kinds. There were frescoes in the Venetian style. There were Venetian arches that introduced and framed water passages. There was a gold-relief ceiling in the spectacular Accademia style of Venice, reinterpreted as a sunburst design. There was a ninety-foot castle tower that afforded a panoramic view of the sea and the sky. There were sculptures, antiques, and bric-a-brac. There were leopard skins on the walls. There were gilded cherubs carved by Viennese artist Franz Barwig.

The original owner filled the mansion with Ming vases, Persian rugs, silverware for two hundred guests, and busts of Homer and Hadrian. When Marjorie Post died, there were nineteen sets of China in the house, each with service for thirty-six.

In the dining room itself, there was a two-tone marble dining table inlaid with semiprecious stones. Its marble top was inlaid with lapis lazuli from Persia, peach stone from Carrara, Italy, red

stone from the Pyrenees, red jasper from Sicily, and white oriental alabaster from Egypt. It was a replica of similar ones in the
Pitti and Uffizi Galleries in Europe. The table seated fifty!

The dining room floor was black and white marble, taken out
of a mansion in Cuba. The room was designed as a copy of one
in Rome's Chigi Palace. Benito Mussolini converted that room
into an office for himself when he was in power. The Chigi Palace
copy in Mar-a-Lago is thus now more original than the original
in Italy.

In the Great Room—actually an enormous drawing room—
there was a copy of the Thousand-Wing Ceiling of the Accademia
Venice, this one done in gold leaf. The walls were covered with
silk needlework panels from an Italian palace. The chandeliers
were imported crystal. The rug came from an old monastery in
Spain.

The drawing room opened onto a closed space called the Mon-
key Loggia, because of the carved stone monkeys perched near
the ceiling. The one seated next to the library wears glasses and
is reading a book!

There was also a loggia in the living room that is a tribute to
the Medicis. Its frescoes are copied from those of Benozo Gazoli
in the Riccardo-Medici Palazzo in Florence. There is a painting
of Lorenzo de Medici, portrayed as the first of the Three Wise
Men.

After investigating the house and examining the details, Donlon reported that the entire structure was in remarkable condition.
The Post Foundation kept a staff to maintain the house over the
years, and it did not even need a major cleaning before Ivana
and Donald moved in.

"It's not as if the house had been closed up," Donlon pointed
out. "The whole house is livable. The walls are in good condition, and the floors are fabulous. There are so many different
styles of furniture, different suites. It's a very interesting house.

"The kitchen is in good shape, too. A lot of people think that
because the house was built in the 1920s, the kitchen would be
antiquated. But Mrs. Post wintered here until the 1970s, and she
renovated things when necessary."

The rooms were refurbished by Donlon in groups, with fabric
swatches sent over to Europe to be copied.

"The house will be kept as Mrs. Post had it," Donlon

announced. Some of the furniture, she pointed out, was genuine antique, but a great deal of it consisted of antique reproductions fabricated in the 1920s when the house was under construction.

"Mar-a-Lago will be [the Trumps's] winter retreat and a place to entertain family and friends," Donlon told the local press. "And they plan to share the house with the community. [The Trumps have] said that the Preservation Society can continue to hold its Preservation Ball there."

There were, however, two add-ons that Ivana and Donald wanted. One was a nine-hole, par-three golf course, and the other was a swimming pool. The pool would be for the children as well as for the adults.

But indeed the acquired mansion became a great deal more than a temporary hideaway for the Trumps. It was Ivana who discovered a real use for the house—as a kind of retreat for scores of her good friends from all over the country.

Within months it became the site of a yearly house party that Ivana arranged for her friends and associates. And at Mar-a-Lago it was a different kind of house party. When Ivana Trump held one of hers, the guest list was composed solely of women—no males were allowed.

"A girls-only weekend at Mar-a-Lago," she called it. "We sit in the spa, walk in the beach, and talk."

And each year thereafter, faithfully, the magazines devoted to the life styles of the rich and famous usually featured a page showing the latest guest list at one of Ivana's Mar-a-Lago parties. Typically the guest list would contain such luminaries as Barbara Walters, Shirley Lord, Anne Bass, Lynn Wyatt, Olga Neulist, Aja Steindler, Iris Love, Nina Griscom, Jane Dudley, Georgette Mosbacher, and so on and so forth.

Olga Keindlova Neulist and Aja Zanoya Steindler, incidentally, were Czechoslovakian friends of Ivana's. Both were married and living in the United States. Steindler had been a former world champion figure skater in Czechoslovakia; Neulist was in the real-estate department of Sotheby's.

Mai Hallingby once recalled one of her weekends at Mar-a-Lago: "Ivana had made up a schedule for each of us, and we all worked like Swiss watches. Then on Saturday night she had in a band after dinner, and all the women danced. It was wonderful fun." Mai's husband Paul was Donald Trump's banker at the time.

Nikki Haskell recalled a recent girls' weekend at Mar-a-Lago—which were usually held, as she said, from Friday to Sunday either in the first or second week in April.

"It's an annual event. Ivana plans the parties every year because she likes to be able to spend time with some of her close friends. She works very hard, and doesn't get a chance to hang out the way the rest of us do."

According to Haskell, "There are usually about twenty women. You get up in the morning, and there's an exercise person who exercises you, then you go to the pool, then you go to the beach, then you go to lunch, then you get a massage, then you get dressed and you go in to dinner."

Sugar Rautbord recalled one of those weekends in a similar fashion.

"Ivana has an extraordinary energy level," she said. "I've known house guests who have had to go and rest after a weekend at Mar-a-Lago. First, at seven A.M., it was aerobics, at eight-ten it was a swimathon. Then someone would challenge everybody in the house to the races. Then they'd have relay races.

"Then The Donald would want to fly to Paradise Island for lunch. Then everybody would come back and have twenty minutes to dress in black tie for dinner. I tell you, they would be white-faced and exhausted, and you'd see Ivana looking simply radiant.

"I don't know how she does it."

According to Rautbord, Ivana has two distinctly different personalities. One is the ice-maiden front she usually puts up when she is in a business situation. The other is a warm, humorous, very different Ivana.

"The public Ivana is fairly shy and cautious," Rautbord said. "The private Ivana is one of the most fun people you can be around. She can be very silly. This private Ivana is extremely funny; she has a riotous sense of humor. She is always telling anecdotes about her and The Donald.

"In a circle of friends, she'll describe real-life situations that have happened in a simply hilarious fashion. She repeats what so-and-so said and what happened here and what happened there—all in her Czech accent. She's great at re-creating situations in a hilarious way."

And that brought Rautbord to the memory of one night down in Florida.

"One night in Mar-a-Lago, Ivana told a group of us sitting around a very funny story about how she and Donald had gone to one of the famous spa resorts and Donald had gotten hungry during the night—and he was furious when he couldn't get room service to send up food."

Rautboard continued the story in an imitation of Ivana's accent: "Donald said: 'I've just paid umpteen thousands of dollars to be starved to death. I might as well be under the bombing Nicaragua. I'm so hungry, and I can't get anything to eat. You can't get room service. You can't even get the *Wall Street Journal*!'"

Rautboard laughed. "Ivana goes on and on in her very funny Czech accent. And then she says: 'I don't want to get the Don upset, so I go out on my hands and knees and I go crawling in the night so they don't see me and throw me out of the place, and I'm looking for radishes, turnips, carrots, because they have a garden there. So I'm picking up all these things,' she says, 'and the searchlight comes on, and there I am in the nightgown, on my hands and knees on the ground picking up turnips and carrots for my husband at midnight!' "

Rautbord sighed. "She was trying to please him and be the good wife, yet she had a sense of humor about the whole thing. I believe it. Her sense of humor is her strength even more than her unblemished beauty.

"And, of course, she is unrelentlessly, extremely beautiful. It's annoying, because she never looks fatigued. She always looks perfect, and she even remembers everybody's name."

Rautbord continued. "Ivana is very sensitive. She takes criticism very hard. I've seen her when she's been attacked by the press, and she gets terribly upset. She's a very nice girl.

"I know dozens of unprintable stories that people who have worked for her have told. But whenever I hear them, I always think: What a clever manager she is that she got them going."

There were occasions at Mar-a-Lago when there were parties composed of males and females, rather than just females.

Audrey Morris remembered one of them held about two years

ago. Before dinner, Morris said, there was a cocktail party out in the patio.

"It was a dullish night," she recalled, "and I was standing there with Donald and my son. At one point, Donald looked up at the tower on the house and said: 'This has got to be one of the most unique buildings. There's no other place like it. You know, when the moon's not out, we even have our own moon in that tower.' "

Morris looked up and saw the illuminated disc that Mrs. Post had installed in the tower so that, as she put it, "on a night when they had dancing or a party in the patio, they would always have a moon even if the natural moon wasn't out."

That was a night when Ivana murmured to Morris in the dark, "I am very, very happy."

Chapter Nine
Queen of the Castle

I vana Trump was pregnant with her third child in late 1983, and it was at this time that the restless Donald Trump had begun to build Harrah's Hotel and Casino in Atlantic City. Although he had not rushed to get into the Atlantic City gambling action when it first began, he reserved a good piece of real estate on the Boardwalk so that he could climb aboard when he got good and ready to.

Now in 1983 he decided it was time to make the move. He had managed to secure a gambling license from the New Jersey Casino Control Commission and he formed a partnership with Harrah's to go ahead and build. Harrah's, incidentally, was the name under which the Holiday Inn Chain operated its casino holdings. Donald Trump would work in much the same way he operated in New York City—using an affluent and enterprising partner to help defray construction expenses.

Ivana was still Executive Vice President in charge of Interior Design for the Trump Organization; going over to New Jersey several days a week was taking up a great deal of her time. And because she was pregnant, she had to take care of herself from a medical standpoint. Much of her time was spent in her usual supervisory capacity on the Boardwalk.

Yet, when it came time to deliver her third child—it was a boy · and the Trumps named him Eric.

And Ivana gave birth with characteristic élan. Nikki Haskell once discussed Ivana's children. "I was there when all three of her children were born. I remember when her last child—Eric—was born."

It was an interesting and typical story. Ivana's doctor got in touch with her and instructed her to be at the hospital for the birth of her third child on a Friday. But Ivana told her doctor that she had an important meeting with the Trump Organization in the afternoon, and that Donald was expecting her to be there. She could not disappoint him; she would be there.

"We went to Le Cirque for lunch," Haskell recalled, "and after lunch she went to the meeting. Then she went to the hospital to have this baby."

And there, with little fanfare, Eric Trump was born.

"I went to visit her in the hospital," Haskell said. "I brought a bottle of champagne. It was around nine P.M., and everyone had left! I walked into her room—but there was no Ivana there!"

Haskell was puzzled and a mite concerned. After prowling around the corridors, however, Haskell discovered that Ivana had gone to visit somebody she knew on another floor of the hospital.

"But she had just given birth about two hours earlier! And she was back at work in two days!"

Eric was born on a Friday, and by Tuesday, yes indeed, Ivana was back at work in Atlantic City, according to Tom Tippett, the manager of the construction job for Donald Trump. One construction worker even made the statement: "We though we'd get her out of our hair for at least a month!" But, obviously, it did not quite work out that way.

Haskell recalled visiting the construction site with Ivana in Atlantic City. "Ivana is a real perfectionist in everything she does," she said. She remembered the week after Eric's birth when the two of them were at the construction site.

"Ivana stood at an angle and studied how the metal beams reflected on the ceiling," Haskell said. "If one didn't reflect exactly the way she wanted it to reflect, she had them go up there and adjust it!"

Ivana continued her efforts to make the Atlantic City Hotel and Casino measure up, detail by detail, to other Trump projects. And then in the end, she was given the job of choosing the color scheme for the hotel's six hundred-odd rooms.

What she finally did was to decorate each of them in a different color. Even though there were many, many different tones and shades—"I didn't think there were that many different color schemes"—she eventually ran out of choices. "I even had to go into grays," she admitted defensively. "And I hate gray!"

"Let's face it," Ivana told a reporter in discussing the conspicuous opulence of the establishment, "people want excitement. They don't want that little black dress anymore."

The casino itself was a combination of hot colors—orange, yellow, red, and purple—sparked off by glittering lights and scintillating glass and chrome. The bounce and glitter of the casino seemed to be the perfect background for a gambler to lose without feeling the ill effects until well out of the place.

It encompassed at least sixty thousand square feet of space— including 614 rooms, the restaurants, the cocktail lounges, the concert facilities, the convention quarters, and the big gambling casino that extended through the entire second floor of the building.

Just off the gambling floor was a cocktail lounge named Trump's, and the main restaurant in the hotel, which featured French nouvelle cuisine, was named Ivana's.

The grand opening of this, Atlantic City's biggest casino, was held on May 14, 1984. New Jersey Governor Thomas Kean was there to cut the ribbon. No sooner had the doors opened, than trouble began between Donald Trump and Holiday Inn (Harrah's), with whom Donald had built the casino and hotel.

In spite of all the hooplah and excitement of the opening, 1984 was not a good year for Atlantic City casinos in general. The earnings estimates for Resorts International, Playboy, Caesar's World, and other gambling stocks were generally being lowered by Wall Street analysts.

"It was a bad season for everyone," Jerry Daly, the public relations officer for Holiday Inn, told Jerome Tuccille. "We captured ten percent of the market share immediately and we were second in revenues only to Resorts International."

Tuccille pointed out, however, that later figures indicated that the casino was seventh in revenue out of ten casinos—not second only to Resorts International.

Donald Trump was not a man to stand still when revenues did not come up to expectations. He decided immediately that he could do better. And he began making his moves without missing a beat. By the middle of August, he was buying stock in Holiday Inn. By September, he owned five percent of the entire company.

Nevertheless, as soon as Wall Street heard the rumors that Donald Trump was buying Holiday Inn stock, the price shot upward. In the end, Trump sold all his Harrah's stock, made a tidy profit on the transaction, and got enough out of that to buy out Harrah's majority in the casino and hotel so that he owned it outright.

Once he had Harrah's, guess what? He changed its name to

Trump Plaza. Helping him in his reorganization of the casino and hotel was Ivana Trump. By the time he finally owned Trump Plaza Hotel and Casino, Donald hired a new manager and became the private owner of record.

Ivana worked to maintain all the interior decorations of Trump Plaza through the daily grind of hotel usage. She continued her walkthroughs and daily inspections, pointing out areas where new paint and refurbishing were needed.

At the same time, she continued to look over her husband's shoulder at the management of the Plaza because she had been with him when he became disenchanted with Harrah's modus operandi. What she gained was an almost two-year apprenticeship at management overview.

Then, in April 1985, fortune smiled again on Donald Trump. Barron Hilton, the son and heir and owner of the Hilton Hotel Chain, ran into trouble with the New Jersey Casino Control Commission. In two months a brand new Hilton was scheduled to open in Atlantic City, but the Commission suddenly flatly rejected Barron Hilton's request for a license to run it. The Hilton establishment was a large one, located in Atlantic City's marina section.

Quickly, Donald Trump set things in motion and quite soon had raised enough money to buy the Hilton establishment outright. It cost him $320 million, but he was happy with the price because he knew the operation would be a big money maker. And so overnight the Hilton became Trump's Castle, to the surprise of almost no one in the world of finance and real estate. After all, Donald was acting strictly in character to name the place after himself.

The next move he made, however, was unexpected—even for Donald Trump. Although, on analysis and in retrospect, it was not quite so surprising as one might have imagined.

For the moment, consider the Hilton—a 607-room hotel, with a sixty-thousand square foot casino, and more than four thousand employees. Like Trump Plaza, it was a huge establishment. Like Trump Plaza, it should be a big money maker. In order to make sure its management was top drawer, Donald made a characteristically "Trumpish" decision—and selected Ivana Trump as its chief executive officer!

Quite suddenly Ivana's life style was changed from a vice presidential function to an executive officer's function—this one the top job in the hierarchy. Immediately, Ivana Trump set aside Tuesdays through Thursdays every week to work in Atlantic City at Trump's Castle.

To facilitate the logistics, Ivana took a note out of Donald's book and innovated a Manhattan-to-Atlantic City commuter run—in the Trump Organization's helicopter. On Tuesday morning she would set out in the Trump chopper, flying the hundred-odd miles to Atlantic City, then back again that night, repeat the trip on Wednesday, and again on Thursday—and sometimes she would stay in Atlantic City at the hotel overnight to save two trips back and forth.

But she worked it out like the professional she was.

Her tour of duty began on Tuesday—a tour that covered virtually every aspect of the Trump hotel and casino business. She would start out on a walking inspection of the facilities, checking for maintenance and making her presence felt among the staff on a first-name basis.

Once the walking tour was over, she would then settle down in her office to review all the figures in the books. She would then supervise the marketing operations, and the purchase of all food and beverages. In addition, she would look into the transportation operations—an essential in the Atlantic City casino business, where large numbers of spenders were one-day and short-term trippers.

From the beginning, she elicited favorable and unfavorable comments of all kinds—the same as she had in her Grand Hyatt and Trump Tower days.

One favorably impressed writer described her and the way she fit into the odd, cross-fertilized milieu of gambling and glamour in the following words:

"Her face and hair and figure are like a casino dream," he wrote. "She is the impossible girl every gambler wants over his shoulder."

Ivana had her own ideas about how she became this casino dream, this person whom every gambler wants over his shoulder. According to her, it took true discipline from the very beginning of her life. "Incredible discipline," she recalled, obviously thinking of her days early in Czechoslovakia on the ski slopes.

Michael Shnayerson in his *Vanity Fair* profile on her, titled "Power Blonde," wrote:

"When someone makes a mistake, she doesn't just say tut-tut, she attacks."

Another employee at Trump's Castle complained that Ivana lacked her husband Donald's tact, and referred to her as nothing more than a slave driver.

"What about the reports that you have just a bit of Attila the Hun in you?" she was asked.

"I'm a lady and I run my business with dignity," she responded. "I don't need to be tough. You get nowhere screaming. Most of the maids can't speak English to start with. If employees are smoking, I call the director of the department. I spend a lot of time walking around the field, and have brainstorm sessions with my managers and solve any problem fast. My managers aren't afraid of me."

In fact, as she put it, "Donald doesn't want a woman in business to be tough."

She went on, "There are a lot of men who are strong and businessmen who are tough, but it's a combination of strength and power that is good, if it is not abused." Ivana felt that in her case, at least, she did not abuse her position, but used it to inspire and motivate.

One thing she learned in her days in Czechoslovakia always stuck with her. "If people see your weaknesses, they will take advantage of them." She hid any weakness she might have, more or less as a way to save her own neck.

On the positive side, Ivana believed in the work ethic. "I wasn't born with rich, rich parents. I was middle class, and fortunately good at sports, and I worked hard in school." That habit of working hard did not diminish after school, either; the work ethic she had been ingrained with since childhood continued to limn her character.

"I just love to work!" she often said. "I always did work. I have a lot of energy, and I just have to do something with it."

More than that, "I like to live. I like to dance. I like to eat. I like entertainment and the family. I like to enjoy. And—knock on wood—it's nice that I can live this way. And if it all goes away, Donald and I, we would survive. We have two hands; we can work."

Fat, fat chance of that happening!

Ivana was trying to understand why many people had taken to attacking her, now that she was managing Trump's Castle. "People get upset if you're really happy. And I think it's upsetting to people that Donald and I have it all: We're young, we're healthy, we love our work, and we have a good marriage and children on top of that! People just can't stand that!"

In spite of her protests about not being tough, that was exactly what she had to be when she became manager of Trump's Castle.

"Yes," she admitted. "A woman coming onto the scene was rough for the men's egos. I was the wife of a wealthy man and was supposed to be in New York collecting art. I had no previous casino experience and Donald put me in. It's like you're thrown into the ocean and they ask you to swim. You swim or you drown. Donald took the chance and he knew that I would swim."

Ivana actually paid little attention to criticism, knowing that no detail of the multimillion-dollar business would escape her notice, and, after all, that was the reason she was put in the job.

"We have over four thousand employees," Ivana said. "A payroll of $1.2 million a week. Ten thousand people come every day to the Castle. We serve thirteen thousand covers—food and drink. It's like running a small city. You have to know about housekeeping, laundry, entertainment, show girls, orchestras, casino lounges, the health club. Plus hotel marketing, casino marketing."

She was very much aware of the slim margin for error in her job. "In Atlantic City, with eleven casinos, it's incredible competition and smart competition. If you make a mistake, it's a million-dollar-a-day mistake. It's a big business and Donald gave me the opportunity to run it. And I'm very happy. And Donald is very lucky I could do it, because it's much better to keep it in the family. This is a family business."

She saw her own qualities of management in a somewhat different light from her peers.

"In New York, I don't have to be strong, but in Atlantic City, I do. But fair. And one thing I learned from Donald is to surround myself with top talent. Some people are threatened by talent; I am not. My biggest challenge is to motivate."

About her job at Trump's Castle, she once said: "If it hadn't worked out, I would have been here for a few months, and that would be that. Donald would have given me a nice gallery, and I could have collected art."

She made it her job from the beginning to sign every check and review every request for purchasing. "Even if you were a vice president," one marketing employee grumbled, "you couldn't buy six pencils for your office without her approving the requisition."

"I run my operation like a family business," Ivana admitted. "I sign every check, every receipt. I'm not tough, but I'm strong. You can't be a pussycat." She smiled. "If Donald was married to a lady who didn't work and make certain contributions, he would be gone." And she laughed. "Show me success without ego!"

"Donald was really in charge," said Dennis Gorski, director of public relations for Trump's Castle. "He was like an absentee landlord." Gorski pointed out that everybody knew that there was a special dimension missing from Ivana's role. "Vision," he said, "control of capital expenses and budgeting for real big-ticket items." And that Donald controlled.

According to Ben Borowsky, publisher of *Casino Chronicle*, a newsletter distributed by Trump Castle, "She was a very different kind of CEO. She was more concerned with the way the place looked and the waitresses' uniforms."

He was once asked if Ivana was as much of a terror to work for as was purported.

"That's what I've heard," Borowsky said, but he felt he should elaborate. "It was mostly that she considered running the casino hotel she was in charge of the same way a New York City luxury hotel would be run." Borowsky shrugged expressively. "There is a major difference. In the casino business, some of your best customers are not the kind of people you would invite to a dinner party. There are a lot of wealthy people who may not have the nicest manners in the world, but you have to cater to them."

According to Borowsky, Ivana simply did not have an awareness of that. "I heard from a lot of people that she was concerned totally with trying to make the place glitzier. Some of these people felt that the money could have been better spent on, say, a Super Bowl Party for certain high-rolling people. That might result in more revenue coming in than having, say, the fanciest Christmas tree in Atlantic City."

According to Borowsky, Ivana "was not focused in on how to run a casino. She was more involved in the way to run a hotel.

Although casinos are in the hotel business, seventy percent of their money or more comes from the casino—and you've got to market your property accordingly!"

That was part of the management problem. But there were more troublesome details. "People on her staff would want to spend money in certain areas. She did not always think such spending was necessary. She was more concerned about the uniforms of the doormen and things like that than she was about promotional expenses that were needed to bring the high rollers in. In the casino business, the feeling is that it's better to give away a room to a high roller for nothing than to rent it to someone for a hundred and fifty dollars a night who's not going to spend any time in the casino."

There was no question but that Ivana was deeply involved in the casino's affairs. "She actually would sign all the major checks like expense checks, herself—everything other than the routine payroll checks. She would even sign her okay for the subscriptions that Trump Castle got to my newsletter."

As for the terror felt by the employees, this was, according to Dennis Gorski, a very real thing. One Trump Castle executive told *Spy* writer Jonathan van Meter the following: "Each Tuesday morning word would come from limo dispatch: 'Mrs. Trump will be arriving in half an hour,' " Gorski said. "People at the Castle would get physically ill expecting her to arrive. It could be a vale of tears."

According to van Meter, Gorski intimated that Ivana considered fear to be her best staff motivator. "Scare them that they won't have a job if they don't perform at peak efficiency," he said, paraphrasing the idea.

Nevertheless, there were mixed reports about Ivana's relationships with her employees. In some cases, she seemed to consider most of the people at Trump's Castle as a part of a large family over which she presided as a kind of mother hen. In many cases, she delighted in looking after their special individual concerns.

There was the episode of the pregnant cocktail waitress. Not long after the opening of the casino, one of the cocktail waitresses seemed to be having trouble getting into her uniform—which was a lovely, form-fitting, and modern cut—designed by Ivana Trump.

The waitress had an out-of-work husband and a child at home, and wanted to continue working as long as she could into her pregnancy. Hearing about the problem, Ivana reassigned the waitress to a more relaxing job in a lounge on the fringes of the casino.

And in the meantime, Ivana redesigned the uniform. What she came up with was a kind of modified clown suit—a court jester getup—that became the required uniform for all pregnant cocktail waitresses.

Carrying out her mother hen functions, Ivana would treat all the waitresses to mandatory makeovers by Maybelline representatives. She would also instruct her waitresses on sweeping their hair up off their foreheads in a modified style of an Ivana cut. They would also get told not to wear outlandish jewelry, or nose rings.

For a woman who was not a gambler, married to a man who did not gamble either—at least, at the table in the classic high-rolling posture—Ivana took a fairly hard line with critics who might assail her as someone contributing to the excesses of compulsive gamblers. She felt that there was nothing wrong with the casinos and the entertainment they provided.

"Yes, the casinos do help the city," she said. "For one thing, they provide entertainment. Also, the casinos pay a redevelopment tax." After all, she pointed out, "No one's pressing the people to come [here]. Some people spend money on drugs, some on alcohol, and some spend it on gambling."

Did she herself ever gamble?

No. "I can't—it wouldn't be allowed. . . . No, it's not in my character. I'd rather buy a pair of shoes."

"As I understand it," Borowsky said, "Ivana would come down several days a week to Trump Castle, sometimes staying overnight for two days in a row. But I think she didn't have the full understanding of how the casino business is different from the regular hotel business. I've been told that she had run-ins with some of the staff—experienced people in the casino business— who felt that they had to fight with her over things that should have been understood."

There was the Paul Patay incident.

At considerable trouble, the story went, Donald Trump recruited the veteran restaurant executive Paul Patay away from the Golden Nugget. Apparently Patay anticipated that there might be trouble with Ivana Trump as chief executive officer of the hotel, and he sought assurances from Donald that he would not be interfered with.

Nevertheless, once Patay was in place, trouble did arise. A *Spy* version of the story mentioned a scene in which Ivana was provoked into throwing a glass ashtray across the table at Patay. Later on, Patay informed *Spy* that Ivana once told him he was too old to hold down a job there.

Whatever happened, Patay was discharged "for failure to perform at the level expected," in the words of the affidavit prepared by Donald Trump's lawyers, and also that he allegedly did not adhere to Trump Castle's affirmative action policies when hiring new employees for the restaurant.

After being discharged, Patay filed a countersuit against the Trump Organization for dismissing him on the grounds of age— a no-no in the jungle of termination rules and regulations.

But the negatives were buried within the positives during much of Ivana's two and a half years as manager of Trump Castle. She luxuriated in the renown she suddenly achieved. There were constant interviews in the newspapers, frequent articles in New York magazines, dozens of pictures of the Trumps entertaining and going out on the town.

"The publicity is wonderful for our business," she once said. "People associate Donald Trump with luxury, flair, success, quality—whatever you want to call it. That name sells. People come to Trump's casinos because of the Trumps. People want to be associated with the glamour, the flair, the success.

"You have to have a certain ego if you want to achieve something. You have to have certain goals. Donald is very colorful. He deals that way. I always say, 'With the good comes the bad.' If you are in the public eye like we are, you are in a sense on the other side. If a story is too puffy, maybe the public won't believe it."

Nevertheless, Ivana included herself with Donald. She, too, was enjoying good publicity, in spite of occasional bad press.

Ivana's job as manager of Trump's Castle attracted the attention of Barbara Walters. She came to interview Ivana on the gambling floors of Atlantic City for a short takeout on *20/20*.

It was there that Ivana's joke about her salary was born. What happened was that Walters immediately spotted three checks that were framed on one wall of Ivana's office. Although Ivana Trump received no salary as manager of Trump's Castle, she was presented with a check for one dollar for her first year's service, a second check for her second year's work, and a third for the current year—to satisfy some technicality involved in salary payment for work rendered.

"I had those checks up there on the walls," Ivana explained, a bit tongue-in-cheek, "so that everytime when my vice president, or manager, or director would come to ask me for a raise, I'd simply say that none of them would be getting any sympathy from me—look what I made!"

It was quite simply a joke. But in Barbara Walter's report it seemed to blow up out of all proportion. Eventually, it evolved into the one-liner that was attributed to Donald Trump on a later occasion: "Sure. I give her a dollar a year and all the clothes she can buy!"

"The papers picked that up," Ivana said ruefully, "and then Donald got beaten up by all the feminists and women's liberationists around the country!"

When Michael Shnayerson interviewed Ivana for *Vanity Fair*, the two of them discussed the successful mix that Trump's Castle, as well as other Atlantic City casinos used, in order to get the perfect combination of low rollers and high rollers into the hotels. Shnayerson called this mix the greatest trick that a casino chieftain like Ivana Trump must know how to perform.

The highest profit came from the high rollers, who were scarce, but spent plenty; the lowest profit came from the poor guys who might spend fifty dollars tops on the slot machines. High rollers were seduced by meals, and deals, and special suites.

The problem was that a casino might woo high rollers too much, paying out more to get them into the place than the casino made in return.

"I would always like to be known as a middle-to-high house, not a middle-to-the-low," said Ivana Trump. "There are people who can come in free on the bus every day, get fifteen dollars to gamble with, and not gamble at all, but just live on this. For them, it's better than an unemployment check!"

Meanwhile, the Trumps were revamping the marina to provide another six hundred slots for yachts for the rich and famous, along with a big new wing and ballroom for conventions and prizefights that would bring in other high rollers and people with plenty of money to spend.

In fact, the Trumps were already winging it with avalanches of publicity. *New York* magazine ran a piece in early 1988 with a long, long list of celebrities and champions of one kind or another who had been invited to fly over to Atlantic City to view the Mike Tyson-Larry Holmes championship fight in Atlantic City with the Trumps.

Names?

How's this for names?

Jack Nicholson. Mohammed Ali. John McEnroe. Tatum O'Neal. Joyce Carol Oates. Cheryl Tiegs. Dennis Hopper. Norman Mailer. Joe DiMaggio. Kirk Douglas.

At the fight, Ivana and Donald sat in the front row. And Julie Baumgold reported the scene on the chopper going back at the end of her story for *New York* magazine:

"Ivana shrugs off her chinchilla coat and crosses her gray high-heel shoes. She carried no bag. Jack Nicholson is in the back with Cheryl Tiegs and the Mailers. With the light on her blonde pompadour, Ivana looks fresh, young, and polished.

"She loves all this, tearing into life, bringing along the different groups, watching their jaws drop. It's a good life, but it must be organized."

And later, "Tomorrow, Ivana says, she will have her hair done, her manicure and pedicure, and then, in the evening, fly her friends to Paris in the 727 [Donald Trump's own plane]. *Women's Wear Daily* will report on her at the couture shows, at dinner with the d'Ornanos and Rothschilds, buying a Lacroix suit called 'Mea Culpa,' for $23,000. But that last is not true. That's obscene. She's a business girl; she'd never spend. . . . Ivana will return just in time to go with her weekend guests to Florida; then, the next Monday, it's back to Atlantic City. Seven flights in nine days."

Al Glasgow, a management consultant who worked with the Trumps, told Michael Shnayerson that it was Donald who handled casino construction projects, but that it was, indeed, Ivana who made certain major decisions and nearly all the day-to-day ones at the Castle.

"This business of signing every vendor's check—no other head of a casino does that. As soon as I suggested it, she latched right onto it."

Glasgow had a certain intuition about Ivana. "You get the feeling not only that she has to prove something to Donald, but that Donald has to prove something to her. She's part of his drive, too."

When Ivana Trump stayed in Atlantic City overnight, she would simply take a quick dinner in one of the restaurants. She would, of course, check up on the service just to make sure it was up to standard. And then she would take paperwork up to her hotel room to check the receipts.

She never got lonely or bored, she pointed out—probably a legacy from being an only child.

Did she ever miss Donald?

"Oh, yes," she would say. "But when I see him after a day, it's better."

Ben Borowsky summed up Ivana's work at Trump's Castle during her two years there. "She was probably used to what the more luxurious hotels in New York would do for certain occasions and how they would dress up their people, and she thought that was important. I'm not saying it's not important, but if you do it at the expense of the casino end of it, that's where you run into a problem. A money problem."

When Trump bought the Hilton and after Ivana had run it for a year, the Castle ranked third among its ten rivals— something considered an astounding feat by experts in the casino business. In the first quarter of 1987, it ranked number one in gross operating profits.

But that was when the going got tough.

In spite of the fact that the Castle ranked number one in gross profits, its revenues had increased only 5.7 percent over 1986, when Ivana took over. But at that time, the overall average for Atlantic casinos had increased 9.4 percent.

And in 1988, Ivana's revenues went up by only 2.9 percent. The average for all Atlantic City casinos was 9.6 percent.

"The numbers were starting to drift," according to Al Glasgow. "Donald runs a business. He didn't like the bottom line. It didn't matter that she was his wife."

"A lot of people felt that the casino could have done a little better," Borowsky summed it up. "Finally, I guess word got to Donald, and he pulled the plug."

And so, sometime in May 1988 Donald removed Ivana from her job as CEO of Trump's Castle.

"She didn't want to give it up," *New York*'s John Taylor quoted an unnamed source. Sometime during the morning on which she was relieved of her duties, she was seen walking through the lobby in tears.

Ivana Trump left her job at Trump's Castle on May 18, 1988. On the eve of May 18, the night before her departure, she and her husband attended an elegant farewell party thrown by the Castle's top management just for them.

"Mrs. T. gave a little talk to us last night," Dennis Gorski reported to the press later. "There wasn't a dry eye in the house."

Then, on the following day, Ivana took her farewell stroll through the casino she had headed for the past three years; and as she did so, twelve hundred cheering employees crowded into the lobby of the Castle honored her with a roaring ovation.

Gorski admitted that the farewell was an emotional one, both for Ivana Trump and for her employees. As the walkthrough continued, Gorski noted that Ivana frequently had real tears in her eyes as she stopped along the way to hug certain employees and engage them briefly in conversation.

"I don't think we ever really knew how deep our love and regard for her was until suddenly she was taken away," Gorski told the press. He seemed slightly astonished at what he was saying.

Ivana Trump was accompanied on her stroll by Donald Trump, who, in an obvious turnaround, walked several paces behind his wife during her good-bye stroll.

"Donald was really letting her walk by herself," Gorksi said. "He was behind her, grinning and watching. Really, this was all Ivana's show."

She left behind a box of delicious candy for each of her employees. After bidding farewell to the mass of people in the Castle's lobby, she held a more private ceremony for the Castle's executive board waiting outside by the Trumps's limousine. There she hugged each board member in turn.

"Ivana's reputation as a stern taskmaster and a tough woman of business has given her a false image as a not-nice person whom nobody liked," Gorski said.

"Everybody is now realizing that we here at Trump's Castle loved her and will truly miss her. I don't think anybody will blame us if we feel a sense of loss now," he added.

Ivana's place as manager of Trump's Castle was taken over by Stephen Hyde, president of Donald Trump's other Atlantic City casino, Trump Plaza.

All in all, it was a tearful and emotional tribute to Ivana's three years at the Atlantic City gambling salon—a tribute that might prove her to be a much more appreciated employer than the grim ice maiden she was portrayed as so often by the media.

Chapter Ten
The Plaza

If indeed the site of Tiffany's on Fifth Avenue was the foremost real-estate value in the Western world, as Donald Trump firmly believed, the second most important real estate value was just up the street on the corner of Fifty-ninth and Fifth Avenue. It was the site of the Plaza Hotel, the center of Manhattan social life in the first part of the twentieth century—and reaching back some ten years into the nineteenth.

The Plaza has been torn down and rebuilt, modeled and remodeled, bought and sold many times during its lifetime; and in the process acted as something of a giant mirror held up to the changing history of New York's high society. Even in the 1870s, when New York began building Central Park, the area between Fifty-seventh and Fifty-ninth Streets along Fifth Avenue was set aside as a kind of deserted space—hence the up-market sobriquet of plaza.

In 1871, the Central Park Improvement Company began building a hotel at the southeast corner of Fifty-ninth Street and Fifth Avenue. The hotel, however, never got off the ground, and in 1882 a syndicate headed by Jared Flagg, a speculator-painter-clergyman, took an option on the present site of the Plaza. But his efforts to build a hotel also failed.

In 1883 another group tried, with a Victorian Gothic hotel rising on the spot, but the establishment was only partially finished, and was never occupied as a hotel. The property was foreclosed in 1888 by the New York Life Insurance Company. New York Life then hired its house architects—McKim, Mead & White—to remodel the vacant unfinished building.

More than fourteen hundred workmen produced an essentially new building in 1890, a neo-Renaissance "box" eight stories high. This became the so-called first Plaza, although a purist could call it the "second" without fear of contradiction, since the original model had been so altered in the refurbishing.

It opened for business October 1, 1890, with an interior typical of the Gilded Age of the Gay Nineties; marble mosaic flooring, marble pillars, French tapestries, silvered ceilings, crystal chandeliers, mahogany and Mexican onyx counters and trim. The new Plaza was simply a clone of the Savoy and the Netherland, which went up across Fifth Avenue in 1890.

At the turn of the century huge New York hotels proliferated: the Astor at Forty-Fourth and Broadway, the Manhattan at Forty-Second and Madison, the St. Regis at Fifty-Fifth and Fifth Avenue—all were more than twice the size of the Plaza. A new consortium of men, among whom was the famous John "Bet a Million" Gates, who had made a fortune manufacturing barbed wire in the Southwest for the rancher-farmer barbed-wire wars, took over.

Henry Janeway Hardenbergh, who had planned the original Waldorf-Astoria at Thirty-Fourth and Fifth Avenue, designed the new Plaza. To make way for its construction, the eight-story Plaza was totally demolished and the land cleared for construction of the building that stands there today. When it was completed in 1907, the Plaza emerged in a French Renaissance style, with enough marble, cream-colored brick, copper towers, and mansard cresting to capture the "in" style of the period. With 753 rooms, it was a mammoth-sized hotel typical of its time.

It faced out not on Fifty-Ninth Street, but on Fifth Avenue. Behind the front was a dining room opening onto a terrace. The utility entrance and lobby faced Fifty-Ninth Street to provide easy access for guests debouching from their conveyances.

In the 1920s, a number of changes were made. The formal entrance was shifted to face Fifth Avenue, and the leaded glass dome of the Palm Court, which was originally a tea room, was removed. Two main dining rooms, fronting on Fifth Avenue, were eliminated. What was left has remained more or less the same from that day to this.

The ground floor has retained the Louis XVI style, with the gilt in the dining rooms, dominated by veined marble columns and wainscoting. The famous Palm Court, modeled after the Winter Garden of the Hotel Carlton in London, still has its "palmy" air, rather ruined by the wall-to-wall carpeting recently installed.

The Edwardian Room, originally a men's cafe but now the main restaurant, is the same, with its giant wooden trusses and mildly Spanish styling. The original Germanic Oak Room, begun as a bar, was converted to a restaurant during Prohibition, with the Oak Bar officially made into "broker's offices."

The rooms on the upper floors were decorated in the Louis XV and Louis XVI styles, with mosaic floors with beautiful borders, so carpet [could] be removed in the summer—a pre-air conditioning wrinkle adapted to keep the guests from collapsing in the excessive heat.

The big opening of the Plaza in 1907 featured the famous food of Eugene Laperruque, a European chef who had retired after working for years at Delmonico's. Upon his return to the States, he oversaw a huge operation at the Plaza that included combination locks on the dumbwaiters and a glass-fronted refrigerator through which guests could select their own individual beef steaks!

The furniture in the dining room and elsewhere was custom-made to the specification of the Plaza's interior decorators, Alavoine and Baumgarten, two famed interior design artists of the time. Even the Palm Court's statues were copies of those in the Pisani Palace in Carrara, Italy, made by Pottier & Stymus. In the guidebooks, they were called "original Renaissance works taken from Italy."

At the time, the Plaza claimed to be the "meeting place of fashionable, artistic, and interesting New York." Alfred Gwynne Vanderbilt was the first to sign the guest book; soon joined by many Goulds, Harrimans, Wanamakers, and Billingses, who naturally took all the desirable corner suites—facing on Fifth Avenue and Central Park—for their permanent residences.

The Plaza's fine location and its posh appearance made it a favored site for big parties and gatherings, especially as the Upper East Side grew in favor and Murray Hill declined.

In 1922, three hundred more rooms were added to the Fifty-eighth Street side of the Plaza. The Terrace Room was created at the time, along with the main ballroom. By doing away with the dining rooms, the main entry foyer and front steps were protected by one of the most elegant hard-top canopies in the city.

In 1926, the Plaza had over a hundred permanent residents, including art dealer Joseph Duveen. With its thousand-plus rooms, it was competing quite successfully now with the 1,800-room Commodore and the 1,200-room Barbizon Plaza.

Tabloid-type scandals occurred in the twenties and thirties to add glamour to the Plaza. The most interesting one was about Margaret Long, a light-fingered chambermaid who stole $100,000 in valuables from guests' rooms. Long "lived in sin" with her mentor-accomplice, Ralph Palmer, a.k.a. Raoul Picard, a well-known philanderer who, unbeknownst to his paramour, was already married.

At the trial, Long shielded Picard until she found out he was married, at which point she said: "Had I known that, I would not have taken all the blame. I loved him, but now I hate him." They both got prison terms.

By the time World War II was over, the Plaza was looking haggard and somewhat jaded. Unfortunately, it had lost its edge as the social center of the city. Conrad Hilton had bought the Plaza for $7.4 million in 1943, made minor changes in the interior decoration, but did nothing to arrest the obvious decay caused by creeping age.

The Plaza's decline had become even more apparent by 1963 when The Beatles arrived there from London to launch their invasion of the United States. Robin Leach, the observer of the life styles of the rich and famous, interviewed the Liverpudlian four at the time. He was unable to keep his eyes off the fading surroundings and wondered what ever was going to happen to the famous Plaza. The answer was—not much, not for at least a quarter of a century.

Eventually, the Westin Hotel chain bought the Plaza in 1975. Harry Mullikin, Westin's chief executive officer, loved the Plaza and everything about it. He supervised an elaborate $200,000,000 renovation of the hotel, and lived there throughout the refurbishing.

The Savoy-Plaza and the Astor died in the 1960s, victims of physical dissolution and economic dry rot. The Plaza remained. Trader Vic's had moved in in 1965. In a way, the Plaza was a survivor in a city of deserters. But it was not surprising that in June 1987 the Westin Hotel chain put it up for sale. Actually, it was the Allegis Corporation, parent of the Westin Hotel chain, that did the negotiating.

Not until March 1988 was the complex deal completed, and then Donald Trump emerged as the new owner of the Plaza—to the tune of $390,000,000. He did not buy it directly from Mullikin, but rather from millionaire Bob Bass and the Aoki Corporation of Japan, two other players in the game, who purchased the hotel from Mullikin three months previously and then sold it to Trump. The deal included $210 million for the real estate, and $180 million for the Plaza Hotel and all it contained.

"When I first moved to Manhattan in the mid-seventies," Donald Trump said, "I'd go by the Plaza nearly every day. Of course, never in a million years did I think I'd once own it!"

What Donald Trump did almost immediately was to install Ivana Trump as the president of the Plaza. She was to take full control of it, to bring it up to par, and then to continue to run it. One of the very first stories that came out after Ivana's appointment as president of the Plaza was that her husband would be paying her "the sum of one dollar a year, plus all the clothes she could buy."

This joke had worn thin through the months—it had first surfaced during Ivana's tenure at Trump's Castle in New Jersey—but it now reappeared in full flower.

A peculiar irritation immediately came from a woman named Mary Bobo in Lynchburg, Tennessee. The story was picked up by the Associated Press:

"On the heels of the announcement by Donald Trump that he has purchased the legendary Plaza Hotel in New York and is installing his wife to run it, one of America's most experienced innkeepers has offered Donald Trump a deal he can hardly refuse."

The story went on to say that Lynne Tolley of Lynchburg, Tennessee, had asked the New York real-estate magnate to send Ivana to this "rural Tennessee hollow." There, she said, Ivana would have the opportunity to learn the finer points of the hospitality trade at Miss Mary Bobo's Boarding House, while also serving as a decorating consultant.

The proprietress of Miss Mary Bobo's was offering the same compensation for Mrs. Trump's work in Lynchburg as her husband had set for her in New York.

"We'll pay her one dollar a year, plus all the dresses she wants, and there are some lovely fashions at the Paris Boutique in nearby Tullahoma," Lynne Tolley was quoted as saying.

Miss Mary's was established in 1908, and had since become renowned for its Southern hospitality and fine Tennessee food served in a lovely wooden building surrounded by a white picket fence—so at least went the story. Although its neighbor was the Jack Daniel distillery, no alcohol was ever served at Miss Mary's because the town was located in a dry county.

"Not even Uncle Jack Daniel could get a sip of his famous whiskey when he dined there," Lynne Tolley said.

A keen eye could detect that the story, which appeared originally on the PR Newswire, was the invention of some imaginative and tongue-in-cheek genius on the staff of the public-relations firm hired to spread around the good name of the Jack Daniel distillery.

From the beginning of her reign at the Plaza, of course, Ivana Trump was in seventh heaven.

"With Donald," she told interviewer Robin Leach in a segment of the *Life Styles of the Rich and Famous* program broadcast June 4, 1989, "You never know what he's going to do next! I was actually thrilled when I heard the news. I couldn't believe it."

She recalled, "It was about February [1988] and I was going then to Atlantic City about four times a week, and it was getting so hard, you know—back and forth and with the children and all." So when Donald told her that the Plaza would soon be in their hands and that he would like Ivana to run it, she told him, "That's just grand. Now I have two places to go to. I'm going to go for four days to Atlantic City and stay two days in New York."

But Donald shook his head. "Absolutely not. If you do that, you're going to—die—it's just too much."

"So," Ivana continued, "when the Plaza did actually come along, I became president and I never went back to Atlantic City at all."

The Plaza, in comparison to Trump's Castle, was a very small operation. For example, instead of 4,500 employees, the Plaza had only 1,200.

Nevertheless, in selecting Ivana as the president of the Plaza, Donald Trump knew he would be running the risk of appearing to set up a competition between Ivana Trump and Leona Helmsley, the queen of the Helmsley luxury hotel chain. This, of course, was prior to Leona Helmsley's court appearance and subsequent indictment for income tax evasion.

The idea was for Ivana to put her stamp on the Plaza without appearing to be an imperious queen, in the manner which Leona was the queen of the Helmsley chain. So, according to Donald Trump, there would be no pictures for awhile of Ivana in the Plaza.

The first step Ivana took on becoming the president of the Plaza was typical. It was simply to scrub down the surfaces of the hotel to get all the dirt out and see what the Plaza really looked like under the dust and grime of the decades.

"The squeak of the squeegee echoes along the corridors," wrote William Grimes in an interview with the Trumps in *Avenue*. "Bathroom tiles are encountering vicious abrasion, and the Edwardian Room's torcheres ('tortures' in Mrs. Trump's Czech-accented English) now gleam after giving up eighty years' worth of crud."

To proceed with Ivana's treatment of the Plaza, each of the eighteen floors of the big hotel was closed for at least a week and turned over to Ivana Trump and her scrubbing crew. With a technical team in tow—including a wallpaper expert, an air conditioning man, a plumber, and an electrician—Ivana marched through the hotel room by room to check everything out.

After the technicians observed and made notes, Ivana then organized a clean team that moved from room to room in a search-and-destroy operation to win the war against the accumulated dirt and muck of the ages.

But the search-and-destroy mission would not be the final be-all and end-all. Once the rooms were initially cleaned, then each team would do eight rooms a day to maintain the newly cleaned surfaces—for ever and ever and ever.

Ivana was adamant about cleanliness at the Plaza. She told an interviewer that there were four elements that made a great hotel. They included location, management, the building itself, and the service.

"I know everybody is sick of hearing about this," she said about the importance of location, "but it is true."

"You know we will spend the money," she said about her management techniques, "and you know we are strong managers."

"It's service that we need to improve, and that will make us a five-star hotel," she said finally. "Service, service, and service. Service sets you apart from other hotels." Ivana and her husband were fully expecting the Plaza to join the Carlyle in the future as New York's second five-star hotel.

Details, details, details. Ivana set up the rules and regulations, which included many details not usually tackled by a hotel president. She wanted all the closets to have padded satin hangers, with towels folded identically in all the rooms. She wanted telephone operators to be bright, pleasant and helpful.

"Put a valet on each floor; give the guests the good towels," she said.

Among the many details that the previous management had failed to personally take care of were these: There were window-cleaning contractors who had not cleaned the windows properly. There were chandelier-cleaning contractors who had not cleaned the chandeliers properly. There were bathroom-cleaning contractors . . . etc., etc., etc.

"I mean," Ivana noted, "the Plaza did not even run the coat-room operation! No wonder there were five-mile-long lines all those years!"

In her role as president, Ivana went about securing the services of a number of architects to provide ideas for the renovation and rejuvenation of the Plaza.

"We did commission about five different groups of architects," Ivana said, "and they are giving us plans for the restoration, especially of the exterior. The sidewalks. The canopies. The door facades. The brass and copper. The lanterns and everything on the outside of the building. It's just absolutely beautiful, and it hasn't been taken care of for a long, long time."

Donald Trump said, "When the Plaza was built, it was built as the best hotel in the world. And it's got the most beautiful suites I've ever seen. It's got the tremendous ceilings, the tremendous molding work, the tremendous everything. Most other hotels weren't built that way."

Ivana mentioned furniture. "We did go to Sotheby's in the sixties, and we bought some pieces—antique pieces of furniture—which we brought back and put in the Plaza. The accessories are magnificent. We have 250 fireplaces in the building, and by putting the accessories where they are supposed to be, it improves the look."

Ivana was true to Donald Trump's notion that the lobby of a hotel had to be its best feature, should act as a magnet to draw in customers, and was the key ingredient to the establishment of a perfect hotel.

To bring the Plaza lobby back to life, Ivana immediately went to work, purchasing brand-new eighteenth-century French-styled floral carpeting, and commissioning chandeliers made of Czechoslovakian Strass crystal. These features were immediately installed.

She hired French craftsmen to create close reproductions of late eighteenth-century tapestries from the Louvre. These, too, went into the lobby, the Oak Room, and the Grand Ballroom.

As for the rest of the hotel, Ivana had the gold-leaf trim on the doorways restored and polished, and purchased Frette linens for all the hotel beds. She also ordered new draperies of French silk and cotton.

During a recent $130 million renovation of the Plaza new tiles were laid on each bathroom floor. Ivana was appalled. "We ripped up the tiles and replaced them with marble."

But one of her first moves, and perhaps the most important she made as president, was the acquisition of Alain Sailhac as the Plaza's new executive chef. Sailhac had most recently helped to revamp the antiquated menu at another of New York's meeting places for the rich and famous—the Twenty-One Club. Sailhac was formerly chef de cuisine at New York's star-studded Le Cirque Restaurant.

"Ivana wants a great restaurant," Clark Wolf, the New York-based restaurant consultant, was quoted as saying. "With Sailhac there [at the Plaza], a number of other New York chefs may follow."

The new chef was hired to focus initially on the Plaza's 100-seat Edwardian room, which looks out on Central Park and Fifth Avenue.

Sailhac brought no revolutionary concepts to his new job. "The Plaza should stay the Plaza," he told a reporter. "My goal is to create a gourmet restaurant in the Edwardian Room by refining what's there." He said that he also wanted to model the Oak Room into a first-class steak house.

Almost immediately, Sailhac closed the Edwardian Room for two weeks. During that time he looked over the menu and studied ways to remodel the hotel's kitchens. He also hired and trained five new executive *sous* chefs.

These five were assigned to the hotel's five restaurants: the Edwardian Room, at the time with a Continental menu; the Oak Room, specializing in grilled items; the Oak Room Bar, which served light dinners; the Palm Court, the indoor cafe and tea room; and the Oyster Bar, with its seafood specialties and raw seafood (sushi-type) bar. In fact, Ivana hired away the famed head chef of the Oyster Bar in Grand Central Station to give life to her Oyster Bar.

"By the end of spring," Sailhac promised, "the Edwardian Room will be a gourmet restaurant combining classical cuisine with the new cuisine, which emphasizes light sauces, natural juices, and fresh ingredients." He said that the menu would be introduced during lunch in the Edwardian Room.

Reaction was generally favorable to Ivana's personnel hirings for the restaurants in the Plaza, and was reinforced later by the addition of a number of pastry chefs brought in from Austria and Switzerland to add a touch of Continental elegance to the hotel desserts.

No longer would the Plaza use canned produce. Trader Vic's was closed temporarily, and, anyway, Ivana was considering changing it into a private club. The hotel would soon be playing host to the finest banquets in the city because Ivana had the temerity to hire Larry Harvey, formerly the catering director of the Waldorf Astoria—one of the Plaza's most energetic competitors.

"I go out with my husband and you get tired of rubber chicken," Ivana said about catered affairs. There would be none of that at the new Plaza.

There would also be new china and crystal. Ivana wanted the uninspired Edwardian Room—uninspired for all its grandeur and prestige—to become a luxury restaurant. She commissioned Oscar de la Renta to design a new floral china for the Edwardian Room.

The renowned Palm Court would become a place for quick meals and low tea, not high tea. Ivana made the point: "There's a big difference, you know."

There was even talk of a health club, installed just above the Palm Court.

It was in Ivana's master plan to keep the sequestered Oak Bar, home to executive rendezvous for decades, essentially masculine.

"The American businessman is going to love it there," said Ivana. "It's duck and steak and baked potato and salad. Good food!"

In another area of renovation, Ivana contacted twelve English designers, each belonging to the Preservation Historical Society of England, to decorate the Plaza's eighty suites in twelve different English country-house styles. These would be replicas made from some of the more exquisite castles and estates in England. Fabrics and furniture would be authentic or newly copied.

One of the first of the American suites to be opened was the Frank Lloyd Wright suite, named for the architect who lived at the Plaza from 1953 to 1959 while he was designing the Guggenheim Museum. The suite was decorated in exact reproductions of furnishings inspired by the designs of Wright.

One of Ivana's favorite fun subjects was the uniforms being designed for the hotel's 1,200 employees. She hired Victor Costa, a Texas designer. Costa's designs were based on Yves Saint Laurent's famous tuxedos, with others based on some of Chanel's designs.

"He's fabulous," Ivana said about Costa, referring to the fact that a Costa dress was priced at about $1,500, compared to $15,000 for comparable couture gowns. "They really take you at those design houses," Ivana grumbled.

Peter Duchin, the son of Eddie Duchin of 1930s fame, and a well-known society band leader in his own right, was appointed musical director for the hotel.

Meanwhile, Ivana was hard at work helping to design children's suites with miniature ballrooms where they could celebrate birthdays and other events with their friends.

In addition, Ivana was designing new bridal suites for specially catered wedding parties, each containing "something old, something new, something borrowed, and something blue."

Ivana also attacked the Terrace Room, the Baroque Room, and all the restaurants and public areas. These would each be refurbished in the best possible manner.

Typical guest rooms would have marble bathrooms, Scalamandre fabrics, and would be exclusively designed by Chanel.

For her floral decorations, as well as all the plants at the Plaza, Ivana hired Eric Jacoby, a well-known floral expert.

She then went ahead with plans to change the old, familiar Trader Vic's into an exciting oriental restaurant, and installed a new health club with exclusive membership—a kind of in-house New York Athletic Club for the well-to-do.

She also resurrected the Persian Room and turned it into a private variety club. It would have as many entertainers as the casinos could provide for it. "It will be the place to be," Ivana said in announcing the reopening.

In her extensive investigations of the Plaza establishment, Ivana discovered eighty square feet of unused space underneath the roof of the hotel, with a breathtaking view of Central Park from the mansard windows. She immediately commissioned architects to redesign this neglected space and form three large, brand-new duplexes.

Ivana announced that the Plaza would always have twenty-four-hour room service; along with one-hundred percent wool blankets, goose down comforters and Frette sheets; private bars in each room; a multilingual staff; beautiful Rolls-Royces; and a fleet of limousines to take clients to their destinations.

"People may not like the tall, modern buildings we have [in America]," Ivana told one visitor, "but the Plaza is an American institution." As such, it was her opinion that it should be kept that way.

"It was scary," she recalled, beginning to work at the Plaza. "There were no inventories. There was no accounting. There were no records."

But she applied her intellectual skills to this new kind of hotel management, and set monthly projections and reorganized the executive staff.

There was one area in which Ivana tried to work something out, but no matter how hard she tried, she did not succeed. The problem was Eloise.

Eloise, to the uninitiated, was a fictitious little girl who lived at the Plaza Hotel; who poured water down the mail chutes, and ordered peanut butter and jelly sandwiches from room service.

Ivana wanted Eloise back at the Plaza. She wanted to re-create Eloise's room and build a kiddie ballroom for the six-year-old set.

Kay Thompson, who wrote *Eloise* in 1955, was not interested, according to Ivana.

"I don't know exactly what it was that kept her from cooperating," Ivana said, "but it's not worth the aggravation."

And yet, Ivana being Ivana, she wouldn't let it go. Perhaps sometime in the future. . . .

Ivana had always considered herself an authority, through experience and know-how, on designer shows. After all, she had been one of the most successful runway models in Montreal before meeting Donald Trump and moving to New York.

She felt that the Plaza was a perfect place to make into the hot spot for fashion designer shows in Manhattan. Within a year, she had appealed to, and had been answered affirmatively by, nine well-known designers who promised to use the Plaza to introduce their new fall lines in April 1989. Nine lines would more than double the fashion shows held at the Plaza in 1988.

The list included Caroline Herrera, one of the Plaza's regulars, who had introduced her collections there for several years already. It also included Oscar de la Renta and Carolyne Roehm.

Veterans in the game such as Albert Nipon, Mary Ann Destivo, and Arnold Scaasi promised Ivana they would switch to the Plaza in 1989, joined by newer firms like Charlotte Neuville, Carmelo Pomodoro, and the Moses Collection by Rebecca Moses.

Ivana missed out on Bill Blass, who decided to stay with the Pierre Hotel. "I love the Plaza, but I have gone to a great deal of trouble having sets and bleachers built to fit the Pierre. I do approve of having one central place that makes it easier for buyers and the press."

Ivana failed to win over Ralph Lauren, also at the Pierre; and Anne Klein Co., Bob Mackie, and Mary McFadden at Parson's School of Design. Perry Ellis, Donna Karan, and Calvin Klein decided to continue using their own showrooms.

To win the coup she did for the Plaza, Ivana promised two full days of uptown shows for each client, using the Grand Ballroom and the Terrace Room at a rate much lower than the competition. She made a point of not charging additional fees for the use of adjoining rooms for dressing areas, as some hotels and auditoriums did. There would be no charge for advance setup time, either, which many designers scheduled for the evening before the show.

"I try to be fair with the designers," said Ivana Trump. "If you have a big function at night, then those people have already paid for the room. Why should I charge the designers who come in later to set up for their shows?"

Ivana was also sympathetic to the problems of putting on a good designer show. "I used to be a model and I know what goes on in the showroom. I know how bad it is for designers to put on a show, what with the expense and with always worrying about something going wrong."

It was Ivana's idea for all the designers to use one runway, splitting the cost among them. That would save ripping out one and building a substitute in its place for the following show.

"It's good for the designers because they aren't wasting thousands of dollars putting up and tearing down a runway. It's also good for the hotel, because all that putting up and tearing down can really beat up the building. A mirror can be broken, or there are cuts in the walls."

Debra Moses of the Moses Collection commented, "We chose the Plaza because we needed a larger space to show the collection and it was competitive with Parson's, price-wise."

Three months after she started as president of the Plaza, Ivana explained what had happened in those ninety-odd, crucial days.

"In three months we have turned the Plaza around," she said. "It is well on its way to its former glory."

She went on. "In my second month here we had revenues of $5.9 million, compared to $2.5 million for the same month last year. Donald and I thought it would take at least until well into 1989 to turn a profit here. We are amazed that the turnaround has come so fast."

Speaking from experience, Ivana mused, "I don't think you can learn management; you are born to it. Managing Donald is a forty-eight-hour-a-day job, then there are the children, the boat, the plane. . . ."

In recalling her first days at the Plaza, Ivana admitted that she was not at all sanguine about making the right kind of improvements at the hotel.

"Quite frankly," she said, "the whole restaurant scene was an absolute mess when we took over, and I knew at the start that we'd have to begin at rock bottom. A million-dollar kitchen overhaul, original mosaic floors to be reexposed, years of grime to be removed from mirrors and chandeliers . . . and we needed new carpeting and draperies, finer silver and china, more formal staff uniforms, better menus, stricter dress codes—there was not one aspect that didn't require urgent attention."

It was indeed an exciting thing to take a brief tour of the hotel, as June Rogoznica, of *Review* magazine did, to see first-hand the "finely polished wooden banisters that were once coated with layers of paint, walls formerly decorated with utility paper, a marble staircase that was sealed off at the ground floor, hand-painted wood panels that were hidden behind dropped ceilings." She went on, "Also discovered were some wonderful, medieval-like antique stencil paintings on the ceiling leading to the Grand Ballroom."

"The furnishings were obsolete," Ivana Trump said. "The kitchens needed to be updated with the proper working equipment. There weren't enough employees to take care of the facilities.'"

But somehow the details were attended to, and things began picking up. For many years, the Palm Court had been a marvelous setting, but it was virtually deserted during afternoon tea. Within three months of Ivana's appearance, the highly decorated room was suddenly drawing a glamorous crowd for breakfast, for lunch, for tea, for dinner, for after-theater supper—and for a brand-new, sensational Sunday brunch buffet.

"We're already having to refuse two hundred people every Sunday," Ivana reported. The number of patrons in the Oak Room and the Oyster Bar remained about the same. "We make no pretensions. Both, as they should, will remain essentially American." Each now had its own individual satellite kitchen headed by its own executive chief. The menus were flexible, but within normal parameters.

"Remember that we're here to give the public the best of what it wants," Ivana pointed out, "like in the great old days of the Plaza. If customers love roast beef and cobb salad, I couldn't care less that these classic dishes might seem too mundane, so long as their preparation is perfect. Then again, if someone comes into the Oak Room or Oyster Bar craving chicken hash or crab cakes prepared a certain way—well, why not? My philosophy about the restaurants at the Plaza is to satisfy the customer, no matter what it takes."

How were things working out now that Ivana's changes had

been instituted and the new order was in effect? Listen to James Villas of *Town & Country*, who wrote in the September 1989 issue about dining at Ivana's newly refurbished Edwardian Room at the Plaza:

"Snapping to attention as you enter the towering restaurant, a formally attired maitre d'hotel bows slightly, asks your name, then ushers you past an imposing silver carving trolley to a spacious table overlooking either the corner of Central Park, where horse-drawn carriages await passengers, or the Pulitzer Fountain on Fifth Avenue.

"There's a soothing murmur in the room that blends peacefully with the old-fashioned piano music, and as you gaze up at the baronial ceiling and admire the lovely flowers and other appointments on the table, you have only one instinctive desire: Champagne must flow, and hang the cost.

"The sommelier discusses, recommends, and begins pouring. After a busboy serves you bread, two waiters deliver tiny appetizers of foie gras and smoked salmon and caviar to nibble on with the bubbly. While the veteran black-tied captain volunteers suggestions from the menu, service plates are removed in preparation for first courses, and the wine steward returns to pursue his duties.

"Now the real drama begins as aromatic fish soup is ladled into bowls, and everyone samples a pristine galantine of salmon, scallops and lobster. Next you confront juicy rack of lamb served with parslied potatoes and buttered green beans, while your companions negotiate the crisp preserved duck, a slab of moist broiled salmon enhanced by an herby zucchini cake, and a fork-tender *medaillion* of veal sauteed with wild mushrooms and artichokes.

"You savor the Puligny Montrachet or Chateau Loeville-Las-Cases Saint-Julien or remaining Perrier-Jouet; and you try to identify the sumptuous desserts presented on the trolley. Then, as the wine and the music and romantic old setting work their magic, your mind wanders to another age. Across the room, you spot a mature couple, she in a silk dress adorned with an emerald brooch, he well-upholstered in a bespoke evening suit and sporting a handsome gold Albert.

"As the spell intensifies, you notice their robust appetites, their laughter, their total involvement in the sybaritic occasion; and

157

when you listen closely, you can almost hear this 'Diamond Jim' Brady as he leans toward his ever beautiful Lillian Russell and whispers, 'God Nell, ain't it grand!' "

Ivana would be the first to admit that her husband's presence at the Plaza helped immeasurably to put it back on its feet. "The Trump name has helped get back some of the old clients and it has helped attract customers. It has come to stand for quality and people know of Donald's and my commitment to making this a fine hotel once again."

Ivana went over her list of special improvements carefully. "We started with the sheets, buying the very best for every room in the hotel. We have also hired a world-class chef [Alain Sailhac] to be executive chef of the hotel. We are painting everything, putting in new carpets, new upholstery. But we plan no drastic changes. The Plaza is the Plaza after all, and we don't want to change the place that much."

Ivana pointed out that she had not ordered wholesale firings of the staff when she took over as president of the Plaza. Instead, she placed her own people at the top echelon and left most of the other employees in place.

She also decided not to push the hotel prices too far out of reach of the average person, although the rooms still run about $200 a night.

"We want to run the hotel smartly, so people appreciate its quality. But we cannot cater just to the rich. We try to cater to everybody, and we try to get the staff to treat everybody with the same courtesy."

As for the all-important restoration work: "We are now studying every scrap of paper in the Plaza library for clues about the original building—its design, the details, the material, the finishes." She said that she wanted to "recapture the Plaza's original elegance," and, to do so, had enlisted two architectural firms for the task: Lee Harris Pomeroy Associates and Hardy Holzman Pfeiffer Associates.

Service, Ivana said, was still the key to a five-star hotel. She said she was training the Plaza staff toward that end.

"They used to crawl, now they walk, next week they'll be running," she said with a smile.

Her husband echoed her about the charm of the Plaza.

"I bought the Mona Lisa," he said. "I mean, look at that—

that's from another planet. It's one of the great works of art. It represents everything that's good about New York. I'd have to say that this is the only deal I've ever done out of pure love for the product."

He added, "I could turn it into condos and make a killing."

A pause.

"But I won't do that!"

Chapter Eleven
Old-Fashioned Ivana

Ivana Trump has been questioned by hundreds of reporters, writers, and radio and television hosts and hostesses. She has been asked time and time again how it feels to be one of the world's most obviously rich women—a woman who is right up in the front row with all those accused by the media and the general public of being the worst capitalist examples of conspicuous consumption.

Although she never answered the question directly, she did tell Glenn Plaskin recently how she felt about being always zeroed in on for an attack such as that.

"What I feel," she told him, "is that [the Trumps] have been attacked constantly [as] nouveau riche. Fifty years ago, the Astors and Vanderbilts were flaunting their money in the middle of the Depression, much more than we do."

She had more to say. "In fifty years, the Trumps will be the old American guard. Whatever I have today, I worked for very hard, and Donald got the money the old-fashioned way: He earned it. Nobody should tell us how to spend it."

When asked once if she thought Donald Trump was greedy, she responded with some verve: "Not at all! He is very down-to-earth in his demands, and in his life style, he's quite simple."

Simple?

Down-to-earth?

Those inappropriate labels conjured up an immediate picture of one of the Trumps's latest acquisitions—the 282-foot long yacht formerly owned by Adnan Khashoggi, the Arab billionaire. Add the yacht to Mar-a-Lago; to the Greenwich mansion on Long Island Sound; to their three-story fifty-room apartment in Trump Tower; to a $2 million Puma helicopter, the best in the world; and to an $8 million Boeing 727—and before you know it, you're beginning to talk real money.

Let's study this 282-foot yacht, which the Trumps renamed the *Trump Princess* after they had purchased it from Adnan Khashoggi.

Khashoggi, who originally had the yacht created to his own private specifications, named it the *Nabila* after his only daughter. Khashoggi commissioned the distinguished British naval architect Jon Bannenberg to design for him the most sumptuous and incredible yacht that the world had ever seen.

"He wanted to build the most advanced big yacht in terms of styling, interior, mechanics, and performance," Bannenberg said. "It was to be the best yacht in the world, and we achieved that at the time."

Indeed they did.

It cost a cool $35 million to build the yacht itself—meaning, specifically, the hull and the mechanism to run it. In addition, Khashoggi hired an Italian designer named Luigi Surchio to produce the interior decor, entirely separate from the vessel itself.

Khashoggi was reportedly paid more than $50 million for the insides alone. That brought the ticket for the craft into the rarified neighborhood of $85 million—just to get the thing afloat.

"No one really knows *what* it cost to build," said Jonathan Beckett, a partner at Nigel Burgess, the London yacht brokerage outfit that arranged the final sale of the yacht to Donald Trump in 1988. That was after Khashoggi had fallen on what proved to be, for him, relatively bad times. The vessel went for about $30 million—a real steal, even after the refit that cost the Trumps somewhere around $8.5 million!

"There are just no words in the English language to describe the bathrooms aboard the *Trump Princess*," one Trump associate said. "They defy description."

The original builder produced a totally self-contained floating pleasure palace, including everything from a patisserie and three-chair hair salon to a screening room with a film library of eight hundred titles. The craft also has a hospital with an operating theater for any emergency that might arise on a cruise.

The yacht has sleeping quarters for a crew of fifty-two. There are over a hundred cabins on five levels of decks. The yacht has a helicopter landing pad and a pair of thirty-foot powerboats.

Cruising speed is 17.4 knots, and the *Trump Princess* can log 420 miles in twenty-four hours. It has fourteen tanks holding 136,000 imperial gallons of diesel fuel; it can travel 8,500 miles—once across the Pacific Ocean, and twice across the Atlantic—without refueling.

Three converters produce 9,900 imperial gallons of fresh water a day from sea water. The craft's six mammoth refrigerators carry a three-month supply of food for a hundred people.

As for the $8.5 million the Trumps spent refitting the *Trump Princess*:

First the hull was repainted white—it used to be gray—then the engine was rebuilt, and 3,500 yards of chamois leather on the interior was replaced.

One of the more resplendent of the cabins was changed into a children's room for Ivana's three youngsters. The hair salon was altered into a cloakroom for guests.

The *Trump Princess* costs them about $2.5 million a year to operate. Its first voyage with the Trumps as owners took it from the Azores in mid-June 1988 to New York on July 4, in time for a huge party thrown aboard it that night.

In the long run, Trump eventually opted not to spend much of his time on the ship. He never was the type " 'as he said' to sit on decks of boats for three or four weeks." Anyway, "it would be too much if I was going to use it personally."

The Trumps leased the Farley Marina on the Atlantic City inlet from the State of New Jersey, rebuilt it, and doubled the number of slips to 633. It was there that the *Trump Princess* finally found an American home.

Quite frankly, Trump admitted that he was making the boat available for selected charities "and" in his words "for very high rollers who spend millions of dollars a year in the casinos." Also, he wanted to make it serve as a profitable tourist attraction.

As for some of the mind-boggling facts about this vast floating extravaganza, there are eleven guest suites aboard the *Trump Princess*, each named for a precious or semiprecious stone with an opulent bathroom with hand-carved onyx and 24-carat gold fixtures and boasting enough lavish creature comforts to keep most guests happily sedated on sheer opulence for a lifetime.

Let's trace the suites through their identifying stones:

On the wheelhouse deck there were the Silver Suite and the Gold Suite. On the A deck, just below, there was the Sapphire Suite. On the B deck there were the Topaz Suite, the Amber Suite, the Turquoise Twin Suite, the Coral Suite, the Lapis Lazuli Suite, the Emerald Suite, and the Ruby Suite. The owner's area, on the A deck, encompassed the Diamond Suite.

By far the most ornate bathroom was the one in the owner's suite, or the Diamond Suite, which contained a grooming station complete with a barber's chair, an elm-wood lattice ceiling, and dazzling starbursts of intricately patterned polished onyx on the floors and walls.

Khashoggi, no slouch when it came to security, outfitted this particular suite with a secret door that could be operated electrically.

"Push one button and you have access to another corridor," one of the crewmen explained. "Push another and the door itself, which is a foot and a half wide, offers a hiding place large enough to accommodate a person."

In fact, the yacht's paneled walls were so well fitted and intricately joined that guests frequently blundered about in dismay, unable in the middle of the night to find the door to the bathroom. For that reason, members of the crew frequently gave guests an introductory tour of the quarters just to forestall any hysteria during the wee small hours of the morning.

From the start, Ivana had her prized room. It was, naturally enough, a bathroom. "My favorite bathroom," she said, "is my husband's because it is a work of art. And the shower is spectacular."

Indeed it was. Shaped like a scallop shell, it was a cylindrical affair chipped and shaped and polished from an enormous piece of black onyx.

During their infrequent stays aboard the *Princess*, the Trumps took up their quarters in the master suite. But when Ivana was aboard on her own, she preferred the Sapphire Suite, which she felt was more to her liking.

"It's smaller and more feminine," she said. But it was not in any way second-rate. The Sapphire Suite, named for its luxurious lapis lazuli touches, featured a huge white onyx bathtub, into which two waterfalls spilled! Ivana found them romantic. Besides, it was obvious that they reminded her of the two most spectacular adornments of the Grand Hyatt lobby and the Trump Tower atrium.

Ivana even had an exercise bar where she could do her stretching routines. Nevertheless, she saved her aerobics for terra firma, but did enjoy water skiing behind one of the two high-speed powerboats that were kept on board the yacht.

Always a stickler for detail, Ivana habitually made sure that her guests were effectively pampered by the floating pleasure palace to which they had been invited. Each bath was outfitted with luxurious white terry robes and towels embroidered with the yacht's logo—a stylized mermaid—in colors coordinated with the jewel tone of the suite.

Other goodies provided by Ivana included a Pupa makeup kit for the women; Chanel colognes, soaps, and bath accessories—scented for the women, unscented for the men; Estee Lauder sun products with sun block; and, for the typical sun worshiper, Bain de Soliel.

Just a simple home away from home for the Trumps and their friends.

As for the yacht itself, it was a spectacle, a statement of astronomic wealth, a massive piece of world-class equipment designed to arouse envy in those who saw it. A friend of the Trumps' was at the helm of his own very large yacht in the Mediterranean, feeling quite proud of it, when the *Nabila* once roared by and practically capsized him.

"He said it gave him a total inferiority complex," Trump chuckled.

Another reason, perhaps, why Trump decided to get that boat at any cost.

Alas! All good things must come to an end. It was not many months after he had purchased the *Nabila*, refitted it, and renamed it the *Trump Princess* that Donald had second thoughts. Perhaps this would not be the biggest yacht in existence. Why not build one himself that would be bigger—and sell the *Trump Princess*?

And so it was Donald's decision to create a $200-million yacht to replace the *Princess*. The new one, incidentally, would be tentatively called the *Trump Princess II*.

Princess II would be 420 feet in length, compared to the 282 feet of *Princess I*. That would make it bigger than a football field (300 feet, or 100 yards). *Princess II* was even rumored to include a Roman bath and an amphitheater.

Also, the new ship would be built in Holland, and not in Italy, where *Princess I* was built. Currently, the most desirable place for big shipbuilding was Holland—and it was there that Trump's triumphant replacement was in the drydock being put together.

Incidentally, the cost of *Princess II*, according to Dutch ship-building sources, was put at about $145 million, not $200.

What would happen to *Trump Princess*? In January 1990 Jonathan Beckett of Nigel Burgess, the London firm that had sold the *Princess* to Donald Trump, advertised Trump's 282-foot vessel for sale in the *Financial Times* of London.

The ad said that the ship pictured in the artist's rendering was "The World's Most Spectacular Motor Yacht."

The price, according to Beckett, was "not for the faint-hearted." In the famous words of J. P. Morgan, another conspicuous consumer: "If you have to ask the price, you can't afford it."

"The price of the *Princess* was substantial," Beckett told a reporter. "The cost of the new one is—extremely substantial."

Beckett pointed out that the *Princess* would be something over $100 million. After all, Donald Trump had already turned down a Japanese bid for $100 million as too low.

Ivana had some difficulty trying to explain the Trumps' decision to build a bigger *Princess*:

"It's not because of the ego that we need the bigger boat. It's a great marketing and promotional tool, and it's for business entertaining. Donald bought [the *Trump Princess*] for $30 million, and he's selling it for $150 million." (The figure in one news story was $115 million.)

According to Ivana, Donald said, "If it [his projected new yacht] can be bigger and newer, and have the new technology, why not?"

The truth of the matter was that Ivana was not completely in favor of the new yacht. In fact, she was not even all that ecstatic about the *Princess I*.

"Well, I'm not a boater," she confessed. "I spend a week on it in the middle of the summer. And Donald has spent one night on the boat. What do we need a new one for? This [the *Princess*] is perfectly magnificent. But these kinds of decisions are really his."

In dealing with the press, a spokesman for the Trumps named Jeff Walker said that the reason for getting rid of the *Trump Princess* and building a new and larger yacht was that the *Princess* had "become too small for the Trumps to entertain guests."

Interestingly, the *Trump Princess* is in the Guinness Book of World Records as the longest private yacht in the world. (It may be simply that the Trumps' guest list also should be included in the Guinness Book of World Records—but it doesn't seem to be available just yet.)

But it was not always only fun and games and yachts with Ivana Trump. On May 25, 1988, she took care of a most important personal change in her life. That was the day when Ivana Zelnicekova Trump stood in a federal court in Manhattan with 141 other petitioners and became a naturalized citizen of the United States of America.

Ivana, along with all the rest, swore to renounce past allegiances to any "foreign prince or potentate, state, or sovereignty."

Judge Charles S. Haight, Jr., welcomed all the new citizens to the "freedom to follow your dreams," and added, "By your presence, America is vastly enriched."

Ivana, the press reports noted, wore an off-white suit, cut above the knee, with a blue-and-white striped blouse.

As the ceremonies concluded, Ivana kissed her husband on the cheek and was embraced and kissed by her friend Jackie Miner, the wife of United States Circuit Court Judge Roger Miner.

Judge Miner, who sat next to Haight on the bench, gave a ten-minute speech on the duties of new citizens. He did not mention Ivana Trump by name, but referred to a special friend who was being naturalized that morning.

"I'm very proud of my wife," Donald Trump said outside the courthouse. "I'm very proud of my country. It's a great country, and that's where a great woman should be. Now they're both matched up perfectly."

Ivana said that she was "very proud" to become a citizen, and called the speeches by the judges "very, very touching. It was hard not to cry."

Outside the courthouse, David Nessenoff, a New York businessman, complained that he had not been allowed to sit with his new-citizen wife during the ceremony because the courthouse guards said there was not enough room.

"I'd have loved to have sat next to my husband as Ivana sat next to hers," said Nessenoff's wife, Julie, a former Londoner.

Nevertheless, the Nessenoffs congratulated the Trumps, pointing out that their beef was with the court officials and not with the Trumps.

Most of her close friends—and Ivana has many—swear by Ivana Trump. It is in fact from those who are not quite so close, but might want to be considered closer than they are, that a great deal of the disparaging commentary about Ivana seems to emanate.

Her real friends love to talk about her—and they speak freely. From these intimate comments, a lot more can be learned about Ivana Trump than can be gleaned from the public prints. She may be, in fact, what she has more or less confessed herself to be—an old-fashioned woman.

And, of course, that may just be a smokescreen to hide the real Ivana.

Smokescreen or not, the real Ivana does occasionally surface.

One day Ivana Trump was on her way to meet a friend for lunch at an exclusive restaurant in Greenwich, Connecticut, when one of the tires on her car blew out. Instead of telephoning the Connecticut Automobile Club, Ivana got out of the car, rolled up her sleeves, retrieved the tire iron, wrench, and jack from the rear of the car, and changed it herself.

"My father always raised me like the boy he couldn't have, or didn't have," she explained. "So the changing of the tire is one of the things that you just do."

Ivana was only a few minutes late for her lunch, and she arrived as chic and spotless as she would have if she had been chauffeured there in a stretch limo. Except, she recalled ruefully, her shoes were totally destroyed.

"I knew if I was going to call someone [to help me] it was going to take over an hour," she said. "So I just put the car up on the jack and changed my tire. It was faster and cheaper. It was absolutely no trouble—ten minutes.

"Everything that has engines, I'm good at. Cars, boats. I had my first motorcycle when I was twelve, and my first sports car when I was fifteen. I liked all that speed and freedom," she admitted. Then she added, somewhat cautiously, "I did mellow by now."

Let's select a few of Ivana's close friends and consider some of their comments about her.

Sugar Rautbord met Ivana sometime in 1977 through mutual friends. They would sit together at dinners and galas, and talk. Then in 1986 Rautbord published her first novel. Called *Girls in High Places*, it got her noticed by one of Oprah Winfrey's producers; she was invited to talk about the book and publicize it before the huge Oprah Winfrey television audience. Rautbord selected

Ivana to participate as a guest when she learned what the producer had decided the show's topic would be.

"The book," Rautbord said, "was sort of tongue-in-cheek, to show that you cannot have it all, and if you're going to be a perfect corporate wife or mother, you cannot necessarily be the perfect stockbroker. Oprah's talk show was supposed to feature some of the real girls in high places, to help me promote the book."

And that was the reason Ivana Trump was invited to be on the show with Rautbord.

"She came because she's a good scout, a good friend, and a consummate girl in a high place—somebody who has a career of her own," Rautbord explained. At that time, Ivana was already managing Trump's Castle in Atlantic City for her husband.

"I saw this gesture of hers as a very giving, generous gift of her valuable time, and an expression of true friendship. She's an extremely loyal person. She flew back to New York after the show."

Rautbord remembered that it was Ivana's first television appearance, and that Ivana hesitated just a little bit before she agreed to do it.

"Oh, no, no, no, I don't want to do this because I'm so shy. They're going to talk about money, and they're going to make me look silly, like we're just nothing but money. I'm a working girl and I work very hard."

Rautbord said this about her friend. "Ivana takes the role of a working woman very seriously. She's a career person. She was apprehensive about the show at first, but I assured her that she didn't have to answer any questions that she didn't want to. I told her she should talk about what was important to her—the business and running the casino."

Rautbord recalled that Donald Trump watched the whole show. "He blocked all the telephone lines," she said. "We couldn't get calls from regular viewers because Donald was tying up all the lines saying, 'That was good. That wasn't good.' He was directing her step by step."

For example, Oprah Winfrey would hold up pictures of Mar-a-Lago, and would ask, "Is this the Trump Castle? Is this the Trump Tower? Is this Atlantic City?"

And Ivana would say, "No, no, no, no, this is Mar-a-Lago."

Rautbord remembered that Oprah was stunned. "She had thought she was looking at a hotel, not a winter home!"

Rautbord is very high on Ivana Trump. "Ivana is a lot more than clothes and dresses. She has a wonderful sense of humor. She's very, very nice. She can cook. She's great with her children. And she always follows through. If she makes a commitment, she does it. If she says she'll be somewhere, she'll be there."

Clement, who knew Ivana very well in Montreal, and who later married George Syrovatka, met Ivana in 1975 at the Audrey Morris Agency.

"I became friends with her because I liked her," Clement said. "She was bright and witty and interesting and interested in many things. She has always been interested in sports, in fashion, and she is interested in aesthetics in general. She has a very good eye for quality, and has a knack for fishing out beautiful things."

Cardinal met Ivana in Montreal, too, where Cardinal was a producer of fashion shows. "Ivana and I are still very good friends. We're still very much in touch. We went to each other's weddings, we see each other at parties, and we still talk a lot on the phone."

Cardinal recalled how she had met Ivana. "Ivana loved modeling. She had met a friend of mine who was also a model. That friend came to me and told me that there was a girl she wanted me to meet."

"She's just beautiful," the friend told Cardinal. "She doesn't know the language, but I'm sure she'll do a good job."

Cardinal continued, "We were doing a show at Simpson's Department Store, and Ivana came by. I knew instantly that she was a natural for modeling—her height, she was a gorgeous girl, nice figure, and, because of sports, she had a great walk. A lot of personality, too. The girls I hired had to have personality. I'm not just looking for a gorgeous face. It's very important that that personality come through in the modeling. I really liked Ivana as a model when I first met her."

In summation, Cardinal said, "I would say that Ivana is a very, very intelligent woman, very good-looking, extremely disciplined. She knows what she wants and is very organized. For some people, she's too organized. They find that she's too strict. She has that Slav aspect—she's a driver; it's this and that and that's it.

She won't think about it twice; once her mind is made up, it's made up and you can't change it. She's always been like that."

In Margo Hammond's story on Ivana in the February 1989 *McCall's*, she pointed out that Ivana occasionally exhibited women's liberation sentiments, even though she has claimed again and again that she is just an old-fashioned woman. Yet Hammond said that recently Ivana had ordered a special pillow that was embroidered with needlepoint in these words:

"Ginger did everything Fred did except she did it backwards and in high heels."

Yet she told the *New York Daily News* that she was not a feminist, even though she might do things from time to time that fit the definition.

"Absolutely not," she said. "That's why *Savvy* and *New York Woman* always kill me. I always stand by the man, never contradict Donald, even though I might think it's silly. I'm a very traditional European wife and I don't mind that Donald is the boss. I like it that way. I have to have a strong man, not someone I can just ride over. This is my upbringing. This is why most feminists aren't married, and have no children. I like to have both. They're never going to get married because they can't find a husband. A man is not going to put up with that nonsense. I'm a normal woman."

In a brief description of Ivana, William E. Geist wrote in *The New York Times* magazine: "[Ivana] speaks with a thick accent that only seems to add to her allure. 'Cowboys?' she says, her eyes brightening and her voice rising, as it does when she talks about most anything. 'We don't want Cowboys! Where can we go with Cowboys?' " She was explaining why her husband bought the New Jersey Generals instead of the Dallas Cowboys back in 1983.

The legend of Ivana goes on and on, composed not only of the good but also some of the bad. According to several sources, she has always had a real fetish about freshly vacuumed rugs. For that reason, all the maids who are employed by Ivana are instructed—not only in Ivana's homes, but even on the *Trump Princess*—to vacuum the room *backwards*, and exit from the room without a footprint on the nap.

The idea for all this is to leave the freshly vacuumed nap erect so that Ivana can walk across a newly cleaned rug and feel the depth and the magnificence of the pile in her toes.

"She's a little spoiled," Donald once remarked.

But about the Trumps's three children—Donald, Jr., Ivanka, and Eric—Ivana flatly stated: "My children are not spoiled. I think they have a sense of reality about money." She meant that even though they have all three been rich from birth, they have not been overindulged like many of their rich peers.

"Donald gets five dollars a week, my daughter gets three, and the baby gets a dollar," Ivana said recently. "They have to know the value of money, otherwise they'll get spoiled."

Ivana has worked out her own system of handling her children. "I keep my children busy, busy, busy," she said. "Every mother knows that idle children get into trouble. I want them so busy with school and sports and after-school things that they have not one minute for—well, other things."

Then she elaborated: "You have to give the children things to do, let them find out what they like and don't like." She recalled that her eldest, Donald, Jr., began taking sailing lessons the summer he turned ten. He told her, "Mom, I would love to get a sailing boat."

Knowing how children's enthusiasms wax and wane, Ivana had the right answer. "It's too early. You don't know if you're going to like it, and if you do decide you like it later on, you're going to have to work for it anyway!"

Because the Trumps are so rich, both Ivana and Donald have been asked many times what they are doing to try to keep the lives of their growing children more or less normal. At one point Donald told a reporter that he spent about four hours a week—tops—with his children, but that he felt he had them covered with that amount of time.

But Ivana scoffed this question and answer.

"We spend as much time with the children as any other parents," she said. "We have breakfast with them in the morning, they're gone until six P.M., we're home when they get home, and weekends we never leave the house without them. Donald takes them to hockey and baseball games, Radio City, Broadway matinees."

Nevertheless, it has been pointed out to Ivana that the statistics are weighted in favor of the children of successful people.

"Most kids wind up in trouble because they're sent off to fabulous private schools," Ivana countered, "or when both parents are working, they have nothing to do, they come home, and they go out on the street."

Ivana had a different scheme, she said. "They don't have time for nonsense. I teach them to be confident in themselves."

As for money. . . .

"If they want something, they work for it," Ivana said. "They don't come to us and say: 'Give me a bicycle.' Even with their weekly allowance, they can't just spend it on nonsense. I'm strict with them."

Sugar Rautbord corroborates the fact that Ivana is an excellent manager of her children.

"Ivana is a wonderful mother. The kids accompany her constantly. On the plane when you fly down with them to Florida, sometimes she will be in the back with the children doing homework, then up front having lunch with the guests, then back with the kids again. She knows exactly what they're all doing in school, and she always makes sure the kids have the right books and their school work. Then, when the plane lands in Florida, she'll get off looking refreshed and gorgeous—and then run a dinner party for twenty guests!"

Rautbord mentioned Ivana and her relationship with her parents, too. "The other thing you have to give Ivana credit for is that before her mother had learned to speak English, Ivana brought her everywhere with her and had her included in all the groups she went out with. Very often, at dinners at their home, Ivana's two parents—who split their time between the U.S. and Czechoslovakia now—are at the table. That's the mark of a very classy lady."

As to how Ivana is able to take care of the three children, and still manage the full-time job of running the Plaza Hotel, Ivana commented: "I wake up at seven, I get the children out to school, I work all day long, I come home and do their homework with them, we have dinner together—no business, no phone calls—then I go out with Donald to a party, two or three times a week maximum. We don't dance until four in the morning. It would be impossible to work the way we do."

Ivana has been criticized by those overpowered by her energy and her self-assurance for being something that most women celebrities are not. Cool. Quiet. Calm. Composed. And Ivana has expressed her own contempt for gadabouts who do not contribute to life around them.

"I'd simply *die* if I were only a social lady," she said. "I could lie in the bed all day and go for facials, but I would simply die if I had only that. For some women, the biggest ecstasy of the day is getting ready for dinner. I would climb the four walls if I had only that."

So would Donald Trump. Ivana's ability in the kitchen apparently leaves a great deal to be desired—in his opinion. Ivana once told the story on herself:

"I used to cook when we had only one child"—that would be from about 1978 to 1982—and, she said, she was "pretty good at serious French cooking from when I lived in Montreal." Yet she said that "I would make these things for Donald and he would look down and say, 'Ivana, where is my meat?' "

Ivana admits that she has difficulty settling down at home after a busy day to indulge in some kind of relaxing recreational activity. For example, reading seems to be something that is not particularly interesting to Ivana.

"It's difficult," she says about this activity. "You come home and your mind is still going, and you put on the television to calm down, and you talk to the Don, and maybe take a magazine to bed, but you're really tired. It's eleven-thirty, twelve—you're gone."

No. Books and recreation are for the summer weekends, when, she points out, the pace is slowed down.

"Gardening? I absolutely adore gardening," she says. "I go up to the Greenwich house, I put the gloves on, and I dig. And I have everything up there. If I do something, I do it big. The garden, it's from here to China!"

There is no question but that Donald and Ivana Trump have managed to work out a very good marriage relationship between them—something that has eluded many other people in the stratospheric tax brackets in which the Trumps live.

Perhaps it has something to do with compromise and consent. As Ivana puts it, "If he sees it the first way, and I see it the second, there must be a third way to compromise. You have to do that." After a short pause, Ivana smiles. "But I'll always support my man."

173

Or it may all come down to energy—the boundless energy by which both these people are fueled, and by which they live in the fast-track style to which they have become addictively accustomed.

Nevertheless, Ivana knows where to stand when she's with her husband. Interviewed on an NBC-TV show called *Women Beside the Men*, she was asked exactly how she liked standing beside the man who was her husband.

"I am a European woman," Ivana answered, "so maybe you'd better say I am not beside him, but just a little bit behind him." Naturally, women's liberation supporters were appalled at this attitude, but their criticisms didn't really bother Ivana—nor do they to this day. Nor does she feel guilty about performing the chores of a typical housewife, even if, with her staff of servants, it usually isn't quite necessary.

"I'm a very traditional European wife," she says again and again. "There's nothing in the household that I can't do, even sometimes better than my own people. That's how I was raised." She has said that she enjoys "fussing around the house."

Ivana has Donald Trump all sized up—at least as far as she is concerned. Hear this: "He's very gracious and if you're good to him, he's incredible to you. If you're bad at him, you're dead." Somehow the Ivana-esque diction in that last sentence makes it all the more memorable and trenchant.

There are a number of charities that Ivana supports, without much fanfare, so that the public has not become aware of any of her work in this area.

In July 1988, for example, Ivana heard about a three-year-old boy in Los Angeles who had a rare breathing ailment. He was supposed to come to New York for treatment, but he was not allowed to because the commercial airlines had no way of taking care of him during the flight and were afraid of lawsuits.

Ivana Trump flew him in on the Trumps' private Boeing 727.

Also, the Trumps spearheaded a vigorous campaign to bail out a widow in Georgia whose husband had committed suicide to save the family farm. Eventually, with the Trumps' money, the woman was able to get herself straightened out enough to go on living.

Ivana has admitted to having felt guilt about all the money the

Trumps control, but she went on to point out that there was a way to neutralize these feelings.

"We try to overcome it by giving incredible amounts— $4 million a year—to charities. I have a guilt that there are homeless, poor people, illnesses, and boy oh boy, do we support them all! What can I do about it? AIDS research, March of Dimes, Multiple Sclerosis. . . . I raised $8 million for United Cerebral Palsy, $1 million for the American Cancer Society."

And so on.

It was only natural that Ivana Trump should emerge in the late 1980s as a definite rival of Leona Helmsley, the long-publicized queen of the Helmsley Hotel chain. It was at the time of Ivana's appointment as president of the Plaza Hotel, accompanied by the publicity garnered by Donald Trump when he said that she would be paid "one dollar a year and all the dresses she could buy," that the media more or less imagined a "feud" between the two women.

Spy magazine ran stories on Leona in just about every issue of 1988, but one faithful reader noted the following in a spring letter:

"I'm disappointed in you, *Spy*. I recently picked up the April issue, and whom did I *not* see in a face-to-face feud on the cover? Leona 'I Don't Pay My Taxes, Why Should You?' Helmsley and Ivana 'One Dollar a Year and All the Dresses I Can Buy' Trump—the respective queens of the Palace and the Plaza. It's such a natural *Spy* cover. Shame on you."

Somehow, Ivana never picked up the gauntlet flung down by this third party. Neither, for that matter, did Leona Helmsley. When Donald Trump purchased the St. Moritz Hotel, however, in 1985—just down the street from the Plaza—and removed Leona from her office there, a natural antipathy between the two women seemed to emerge at least in the minds of the media manipulators.

Feud? Not really. But indeed Ivana Trump was taking control of the Trump hotels in much the same manner that Leona Helmsley had taken control of the Helmsley hotels. The feud, according to Michael Moss's book *Palace Coup*, was subdued and unstated. He referred to the fact that in several of the Helmsley executive offices there were cartoons on the walls referring to the Trumps. One showed the skyline of Forty-second Street in

Manhattan and the word Trump plastered over a dozen buildings—except for the Helmsley Hotel, which was labeled No Trump.

At Trump dinners and Helmsley dinners no one mentioned Helmsley or Trump, in that order. But it was obvious that the two women had very different styles and tastes; these clashed, but, disappointingly, not the individuals behind them.

But it was Donald and Leona who were the real feuders—not Ivana and Leona. At Donald Trump's huge Fourth of July weekend party held aboard the *Trump Princess* in 1988, the extensive invitation list did not include the Helmsleys—and it was Leona's birthday!

About the fact that soon she might well turn out to be the biggest woman in the hotel business, what with Leona Helmsley out of the picture for the foreseeable future, Ivana had this to say:

"I don't jump from project to project. I want to finish what I have begun at the Plaza. If Donald will want me [at the Taj Mahal in Atlantic City—Trump's newest acquisition] I would go, but I don't want to be jumping. I wasn't passed by."

As for running a hotel empire, Ivana was not at all eager to extend herself in that direction. "I don't think so," she said. "I don't want to have fifteen different hotels, because I like to be very hands-on. Donald is different; he can work on twenty projects. I'm not saying I'm going to be at the Plaza for the next hundred years. Maybe Donald is going to buy something else."

Ivana Trump created somewhat of a furor in 1988 when she suddenly opted out of her regular Boeing 727 flights to Paris to visit the designers and buy new outfits. Her statement was that she would in the future forego Paris for New York—in other words, forsake French for American design.

That resolve lasted about a year.

By the middle of 1989, she was ready to take a shot at Paris once again. And in July she was in the City of Light at a dinner held by Brigitte de Ganay at Paris's Plaza Athenee.

Not every woman can wear those ferociously sexy Ungaros, she commented, adding, "with a good body like mine you don't really need to wear made-to-measure."

She said that she would purchase some Givenchy and Dior

items—Givenchy and Dior being the two designers whose pant-suits served as uniforms for the Trumps' Atlantic City employees.

"I won't start buying publicly," she told reporters. "They'll come to me." She was referring to the fact that the Plaza would soon have more designers giving fashion shows in her hotel—particularly Parisian ones. "They stay in our hotels and they have a great time." And that would cut down an appreciable amount on Ivana's flying expenses. "I could buy five more dresses for the $100,000 it costs me to bring my plane to Paris."

For Ivana, flying was not really her favorite mode of transportation.

"Donald takes the helicopter to the Greenwich weekend house [from New York], but I'd rather drive there in my little red Ferrari."

Chapter Twelve
The Unforgettable Woman

When Donald Trump designated Ivana Trump to be manager of Trump's Castle in Atlantic City in 1985, it marked a definite change in her life style. And, apparently, it also marked a definite change in the life style of Donald.

With Ivana now plunged into a full-time job—and a big one—in addition to keeping the children in line and making sure that her homes were well run, she had little time to spend tagging along after her husband.

Tracing the activities of Ivana and Donald at the time, it becomes obvious that they soon began to drift apart—both as lovers and as husband and wife. Ivana's responsibilities at Trump Castle required her presence in Atlantic City from Tuesday through Thursday. Donald, on the other hand, sometimes went down to Atlantic City for the weekend.

And so Ivana was there during the week, Donald over the weekend. The time they were spending together was growing less and less.

In a *New York* magazine article, John Taylor quoted a friend who said of Donald: "He talked about girls all the time. He would say, 'I can't believe I'm married. This is the prime time for me.' "

In other words, why wasn't he availing himself of the opportunity of playing around?

On the other hand, Ivana's friends pointed out that she was quite happy with her new life style. One said: "It worked well with Ivana for a long time. She was willing to have a relationship where she got nothing emotionally. Her own needs were less than the average person's, and she had the external trappings, the tremendous social presence and visibility."

Ivana had her own busy life to attend to. Donald had his too, but his new freedom gave him more time to pursue his own expressed interest in girls. His social life expanded noticeably and he became much more active—almost as much as in his bachelor days in Manhattan when he was quite a swinger.

Whatever the truth of the matter was, rumors soon began surfacing in the large circle of friends around him about a number of newfound acquaintances—usually of the opposite sex. Apparently these rumors reached the ears of Ivana, but if she was at all distressed by them, she never allowed her inner turmoil to surface in public.

The Trumps were discreet enough to keep any of their possible spats out of the press and hidden from the prying eyes and cameras of the electronic media.

Yet the rumors persisted, and finally they began to be spiced up with names.

There was Catherine Oxenberg, a television actress who played in the prime-time soap *Dynasty*.

There was Carol Alt, a professional model.

There was even Olympic ice skater Peggy Fleming.

There was cosmetics queen Georgette Mosbacher, wife of Secretary of Commerce Robert A. Mosbacher.

There was fashion designer Carolyne Roehm, married to business tycoon Henry Kravis.

And, in addition, there was even Robin Givens, another television actress from the series *Head of the Class*.

One of the most bizarre elements in this grab bag of possible other women was the fact that two of the most frequently mentioned—Georgette Mosbacher and Carolyne Roehm—were close friends of Ivana's. But that was the way the gossip mills ground in those months of the late 1980s. It seemed that almost any woman who shook hands with Donald Trump was suspect.

It was even bandied about among the fourth estate that Donald had been known to relish reports of his supposed flirtations with the wives of his rivals. In fact, Donald let it be known in 1989 that he was being pursued by a former model, the wife of Hartz Mountain tycoon Leonard Stern. Of course, this started a series of denials, which Donald fanned into flames when he quite recently fended off a *Playboy* interviewer's questions about his taste for monogamy.

"What is marriage to you?" asked Glenn Plaskin, who was conducting the interview for the January 1990 issue of *Playboy*. "Is it monogamous?"

"I don't have to answer that," Donald responded quietly. "I never speak about my wife—which is one of the advantages of not being a politician. My marriage is and should be a personal thing."

"But you do enjoy flirtations?" Plaskin persisted.

"I think any man enjoys flirtations, and if he said he didn't, he'd be lying, or he'd be a politician trying to get the extra four votes. I think everybody likes knowing he's well responded to. Especially as you get into certain strata where there is an ego involved and a high level of success, it's important. People really like the idea that other people respond well to them."

In other words, unless a person had to depend on his public image, he should do exactly what his libido urged him to do. A male, Donald seemed to be saying, was essentially polygamous; a successful male was thus entitled to greater latitude in his polygamous encounters in line with the medieval system of droit du seigneur—the right of the lord of the manor to the sexual favors of the vassal's bride on her wedding night.

"How is your marriage?"

"Just fine. Ivana is a very kind and good woman. I also think she has the instincts and drive of a good manager. She's focused and she's a perfectionist."

"And as a wife, not a manager?"

"I never comment on romance. . . . She's focused and she's a great mother, a good woman who does a good job."

Not exactly a glowing tribute to Ivana's sex appeal.

In the list of names tossed about by the media as possible intimates of Donald Trump there was one name that seemed conspicuously absent: that of Marla Maples. Marla had been born in a Georgia town quaintly named Tunnel Hill, and grew up in nearby Dalton. In her younger days—she was twenty-six when the story linking her with Donald Trump broke in February 1990—she was the homecoming queen at Whitfield County's Northwest High School.

Graduating in 1981 as one of the top twenty in a class of four hundred, she enrolled at the University of Georgia, majoring in marketing, and then quit to become a flight attendant for Delta Airlines for a short time. She began doing the rounds of the beauty contest circuit after that, taking part first in a bikini contest in Daytona, Florida, in 1983, which she lost.

In 1984 she was named the Miss Resaca Beach Poster Girl in a beauty contest named for a small town near Dalton. Later, she competed for the title of Miss Hawaiian Tropic, a suntan lotion. She lost that, too, but on the strength of her looks, was urged to enter the Miss Georgia-U.S.A. contest by Jerry Argovitz, a football agent and then part owner of the Houston Gamblers football team, and later manager of the New Jersey Generals of the U.S. Football League—soon to become the property of Donald Trump.

She lost the Miss Georgia contest, too but, got a bit part in a Dino De Laurentiis movie largely through the help of Argovitz. She then moved to New York to make the rounds of the model agencies. Her book was accepted by the Ford Modeling Agency—one of New York's top agencies. Her modeling career was not too impressive, but she did appear on a Delta Airlines billboard and in advertisements for Miracle Ceramic Tile Adhesive.

"She's a sweet innocent kind of girl," one producer said. "But she had a problem doing commercials. She has innocence but incredible sexiness that bothers advertisers. She's like an old-time glamour girl."

She became interested in motion picture roles, particularly after her debut with Dino De Laurentiis, and appeared in Stephen King's 1986 movie, *Maximum Overdrive*, with Emilio Estevez, as the second woman; and as the tennis player in Herbert Ross's 1987 film, *The Secret of My Success*, starring Michael J. Fox. Neither picture was a huge hit. *Overdrive* was assessed by Leonard Maltin as a "junk movie . . . stupid and boring" and *Secret* as "too long."

In New York in May 1987, Marla decided to join the Marble Collegiate Church. At the time, she was living with Thomas Fitzsimmons, a former policeman turned model, and the producer mentioned above. Fitzsimmons had also been a friend of Donald Trump during Donald's bachelor days in Manhattan. He and Marla lived in a trendy East Side high-rise studio apartment close to the United Nations.

Marla was a big fan of Dr. Norman Vincent Peale, and even though Peale was about to give up his ministry there—to be succeeded by Dr. Arthur Caliandro—she persuaded Fitzsimmons to attend Sunday services with her.

Although Donald Trump had been married to Ivana in Marble

Collegiate, he had never become an actual member of the congregation. Ivana did not particularly care to go to and be seen in church, and when Donald did go, he usually went alone. Besides, Ivana was a Roman Catholic.

It was presumably at Marble Collegiate that Donald met Marla, then on the arm of Thomas Fitzsimmons, his friend from the past. Or he could have met her at a party. Anyway. . . .

No details are known as to what actually happened, but it is known that around Christmas time in 1988—when all those rumors about trouble between Donald and Ivana were surfacing in the press—he sought religious counseling from Dr. Caliandro at Marble Collegiate.

"He was quite broken up," one source was quoted as saying, having become emotionally torn between his relationship with Marla and his marriage obligations to Ivana.

And the rumor mills continued to grind. The media—fed with bits and pieces by intimates of the Trumps—knew something was bubbling below the surface, but no one in the fourth estate could put a definite finger on anything factual to justify coming out with the story.

Deborah Mitchell, a writer for the New York weekly 7 *Days* once complained to a colleague that she would periodically get what she considered to be a real tip on a Trump story, but as soon as she reported it, she would get denials. Sources that had *seen* something firsthand would suddenly develop amnesia, saying that what they had seen was no more than hearsay. Every tip would simply dissipate into smoke.

On October 10, 1989, three top executives of Trump Enterprises met with Donald in his office in Trump Tower for a routine meeting. When they rose to fly back to Atlantic City one asked him, "Are you coming down with us?"

"You know," Donald told them, "I'm just too busy."

And so Stephen Hyde, who had replaced Ivana at Trump's Castle in Atlantic City, Mark Grossinger Etess, president of the Taj Mahal casino project, and Jonathan Benanav, executive vice president of the Trump Plaza, walked out of the Tower to board a helicopter for Atlantic City.

On its way to New Jersey it crashed, killing all three men and the two pilots.

One hour later, Donald got a telephone call from a television station. "Five dead," said the voice on the wire. "You have any comment?"

Donald was stunned. There, but for the grace of God. . . .

Ivana took it even harder than Donald. "A tragedy," she told Glenn Plaskin later. "Really brought my life into perspective. One day you're here, the second day you're gone. What you achieve really doesn't mean a thing. What really matters is your family, not your work, not your possessions, not a boat, not a story in the newspaper. It just doesn't mean a thing. It's my family."

The three men were friends of hers. "I cried and cried for days and weeks. I'm Christian and do believe in God, that we go somewhere . . . it gives me a sense of hope. It does, it does. Two of them were married. . . . What could I say to their wives? It was just a catastrophe. Donald and I went over, we hugged and kissed them. Then, those women sit alone. This is when you really get lonely."

Donald's reaction was dramatically different from Ivana's. He told John Taylor later the manner in which the incident affected him and his philosophical attitude about living.

"It cheapened life to me, unfortunately," he said. "These were three incredibly vibrant guys. It tends to cheapen life when you see quality like that going for no reason. It's truly a horrible experience."

Donald's sudden intuition of the transitory nature of life was a revelation—and a catalyst for the months that lay ahead. After all, Hyde was forty-three, Etess thirty-eight, and Benanav only thirty-three. Donald Trump realized that if life was so easily snuffed out, it behooved a man or a woman to live it to the hilt, to enjoy every second of it while it lasted.

"I'm always looking for more excitement in life," he told Connie Chung in a television interview made a few months after the helicopter crash. "I look at life as one time, here we are, it's a one-time go-around." He told her how his mega-deals fueled that kind of personal excitement. "There's a level of importance there that, I think, also somewhat turns me on."

When she asked him if he thought he had gone through his mid-life crisis yet, he responded: "I think I [have]. . . . I don't think from my standpoint it's been a particularly dramatic period." Then, reconsidering it carefully, he added, "Maybe I haven't been there yet. If I do go through a mid-life crisis, I'll call you. It'll be very exciting."

Prophetic words.

But that's getting ahead of the story. All through 1989 the bubbling, bubbling, toiling and troubling continued. To back up a bit, in late spring 1989 a story appeared that seemed to be simply an opening salvo in what might be termed the Silly Season in journalism. One of the first writers to get into the fray was Anne L. Adams, a staff writer at the *New York Daily News*. She zeroed in on Ivana in a somewhat circumspect manner.

"There was something different about Ivana on Friday night," she said in her lead for May 14, 1989. "Something, ah, more."

Note that she was actually saying nothing specific—just expressing a feeling, a hint, a soupcon of, well, suspicion.

The story went on to imply that perhaps Ivana Trump had not been seen for four weeks or more—an unusual thing in New York—for some specific reason. There were several guesses:

"Some said she went underground after *Spy* magazine's recent [May 1989], rather acid 'tribute.' Others speculated she had gone for treatments of one sort or another." The wording of the second sentence throbbed with innuendo. The Plaza Hotel public relations office simply noted that she was buried under a pile of work.

At the Police Athletic League SuperStar dinner May 12, 1989, she reappeared, as Anne Adams wrote, but—was it really Ivana? Were the eyes the same? Wasn't the nose just a bit more pert? Did not her model's figure seem—well—more voluptuous? Or was it the décolletage of the dress?

It was generally assumed by the media that Ivana actually did go under the knife, in the offices of a well-known Beverly Hills plastic surgeon, for a face-lift and breast-lift.

Ivana's personal secretary, Jan Kovach, responded to media questions with the story that Ivana had "completely, completely changed her makeup." She was going in for softer, paler shades, and her hair was not quite so lacquered.

All kinds of then and now pictures appeared side by side, comparing the two Ivanas—and, yes, indeed, it did seem that she had changed her makeup styling, toned it down a bit, if you would.

"I changed from dark, dramatic colors to peaches and pinks,"

Ivana told *Longevity* magazine. And she had started working out three mornings a week with a personal trainer.

Even by the end of the year 1989 the media refused to let the story alone.

"No. No plastic surgery," Ivana told *USA Today* after persistent questioning. "Why? Do I look like I've had plastic surgery?"

USA Today noted that indeed she did look as if expert fingers had taken a tuck or two here and there. The wrinkles around the eyes and excess chin folds that had been apparent in a 1988 photo were simply not evident in pictures taken in 1989.

Ivana shrugged. "I got rid of all my makeup. I gave it to my housekeeper. I went from reds to pinks, from rust to beige. I let my hair grow and I let it be straight."

Also, she said that she had lost weight through the three-times-a-week workouts she had mentioned.

"You come into a certain age and you know less is more."

Visiting Fred Hayman's and Giorgio's on Beverly Hills's Rodeo Drive on a shopping tour in December 1989 with a husky body-guard, Ivana was noticed and dissected by the local aristocracy. "Her look was nice," one commentator said within earshot of a reporter, "but in that poufed and sprayed New York way. Not the natural, Beverly Hills way."

About the gossip over the possibility of plastic surgery, Ivana noted how she felt about a face-lift:

"Nothing wrong with it. I believe that if you can improve yourself in any way, you should do it if you have the money. Some people don't care what they wear—intellectual growth is most important to them, and that's fine. But if you like to feel and look good, and I do, it's a whole package of putting yourself together."

She had once said that she never intended to look a day over twenty-eight years of age, but that it was going to cost Donald Trump a lot of money. Had she meant that she was contemplating plastic surgery?

"I'm not going to comment one way or the other. If people can improve themselves, they should. If they can do it with their hairdo and makeup, great. If they can't, if they need plastic surgery, that's fine, too."

Whatever improvement the plastic surgery was supposed to

achieve in her personal life, it apparently did not do the trick she had hoped it would.

The rumor mills began to grind faster and faster, and as they increased in speed, they increased also in decibels. But still Ivana pursed her lips and let out not a murmur. It was as if everything in life were chugging along as natural as could be.

According to her close friends, she was keeping a stiff upper lip and pretending everything was all right. Because of course everything was not all right. She was being wronged, and she was aware that she was being wronged—but she chose to do nothing about it.

In her mind it was more wrong to spill out all one's feelings and frustrations to close friends than simply to bottle it all up and suffer it in silence.

Actually, the affair had been going on for some time before the rumors began to surface. It has now been ascertained that Marla Maples was living at a luxury suite at the St. Moritz Hotel about mid-1987, apparently just after the relationship began. Donald had purchased the St. Moritz from Harry Helmsley in 1985, and, since Ivana was working every day at Trump's Castle in Atlantic City, Donald had plenty of latitude to be with Marla in Manhattan whenever he chose.

Investigative reporters dug up a number St. Moritz employees who claimed to have seen Donald in hotel suite No. 414, which was assigned to Marla Maples. Donald would be accompanied by his bodyguard, the story went, and the bodyguard would then station himself outside the main hotel entrance to watch out for Ivana or other unwanted visitors.

Then, when Ivana was put in charge of managing the Plaza Hotel just down the street from the St. Moritz, Donald changed his visits to a few hours instead of overnight.

"I saw Trump in the room with Marla on three occasions," one unnamed employee said. "One time he had on a beautiful silk robe that looked Oriental."

In February 1988 Trump sold the St. Moritz. He then moved Marla elsewhere—either to a Sixty-eighth street apartment, or to the Waldorf Towers on Park Avenue, the residency part of the Waldorf Hotel, depending on your source of information. Later she occupied a suite in Trump Castle, obviously after Ivana had been assigned to the Plaza Hotel.

All was not complete sweetness and light in this relationship, according to witnesses. Apparently Donald assigned a number of guards to Marla, ostensibly to protect her from the press and curious onlookers. Called the Corvette Squad, this twenty-four-hour security service was established for one purpose only: to keep Marla well within sight at all times and to make sure Marla and Ivana never met face-to-face.

Temper tantrums were a frequent diversion, members of the Corvette Squad claimed. Donald banned Marla from the *Trump Princess* when Ivana was aboard, and Marla did not like to be banned.

She stormed around her suite at Trump Castle one time when she was angry, kicking at the furniture and everything in sight. Her foot was injured and she had to hobble around on crutches for about three weeks.

Marla was also infuriated when she was not allowed to watch a boat race from the *Trump Princess* in September 1989 because Ivana was on board.

By the summer of 1989, Ivana had not yet heard any specific information about Marla Maples and of The Donald's attachment to her, yet she and Donald had apparently already come to a rather serious parting of the ways. There were quarrels and accusations, according to friends. There was also, apparently, a separation or two.

In order to determine what her rights were, Ivana made a discreet visit to divorce attorney Raoul Felder in early 1989, during one of the Trumps' periodic separations, for a consultation about her situation.

Soon after that visit, the Trumps reconciled once again.

And it looked as if the marriage had been cemented together.

Until Christmas 1989 when everything fell apart.

The Trumps had always enjoyed their winter weekends in Aspen, Colorado, on the ski slopes. It was a kind of trip down memory lane, reminding them of their first months together before they were married and when they were deeply in love.

On schedule, Ivana flew out to Aspen a day before her husband. Ensconced in her Aspen dwelling, she did not greet him at the airport when he flew in. Apparently he brought Marla with him.

The holiday season started out as usual for Ivana, with an occasional run down the slopes with Donald. But then, abruptly, things changed dramatically.

A shocked Ivana was called aside on December 29 by several close friends who began talking to her. They told her that Donald's other woman was actually at Aspen. Ivana was stunned. Her friends soon pointed out the woman in question. Ivana had seen her before, of course, but she had never tied her up with Donald. Somewhere—at a party? At a dinner? One of the many.

Ivana did not know it, but Donald had been indulging in the age-old Hollywood beard game; a man and his mistress, with a third male pretending to squire the mistress, and known as the beard. Thus had Marla Maples been hidden.

Taking furious note of the woman, Ivana realized subconsciously that Marla Maples was almost a dead ringer for herself—with, of course, the advantage of some ten years on her.

Donald Trump's wife found herself in a peculiar and unenviable position. For at least three years she had known that Donald was playing around with other women, and because she thought she understood him, she ignored his secret conquests, feeling that they were transitory and would soon fade away.

Now, for him to flaunt this woman in front of her—during their sentimental holiday season at Aspen!—that was the end of any silence she might have imposed on herself.

Worse than Donald's open womanizing was the sudden move put on Ivana by Marla herself.

Two days later, on December 31, as Donald and Ivana were putting on their skis in front of Bonnie's famous Mid-Mountain Restaurant in Aspen, halfway down Ajax Mountain at the top of the Little Nell lift, they were suddenly confronted by Marla Maples.

"Are you in love with your husband?" Marla was said to have challenged Ivana. "Because I am."

Stunned at the suddenness of the attack, Ivana finally found her tongue and responded. "You bitch, leave my husband alone!" she ordered in no uncertain terms.

"I love him," Marla persisted, "and if you don't, why don't you let him go?"

"You stay away from my husband—or else!" snapped Ivana, and then suddenly lost her icy Czech cool and went up in flames.

One witness said that she began cursing Marla and was so angry she couldn't even pronounce her name right. She keep calling her "Moo-lah." As for Donald, he simply sat there, lacing up his skis, until the storm subsided and Marla backed off and left the scene.

With his characteristic coolness, Donald turned to his enraged wife. "You're overreacting," he told her. Then, with a very bemused smile, he took off down the side of the mountain on his skis.

What happened after that was one of those once-in-a-lifetime real-life incidents that would seem ridiculous even in a Golden Age of Television screwball comedy. Ivana shot out after him, passed him up easily with her superior downhill technique, flipped around 180-degrees to ski backwards in front of him all the way down the slope, wagging her finger in his face like a mother scolding a fractious child.

That night, on New Year's Eve, it was reported that Donald took Marla, not Ivana, to a huge party thrown by David Koch, the oil-industry billionaire.

Koch answered the phone later when the party was in full swing. It was Ivana. She asked him if Donald was there with his girlfriend.

The oilman knew there was trouble brewing between the two strong-minded Trumps. He had no idea how to handle the situation. Instead, he laughed nervously, unable to come up with a suitable comeback. Ivana interpreted that braying burst of nerves to mean that he was laughing at her.

"That was the straw that broke the camel's back," a witness said. Ivana took it to mean that, like Koch, everybody was laughing at her.

The upshot of all this was that Ivana vanished from sight for several days, sitting in her room heartbroken and depressed.

Because of this bizarre confrontation with Marla, Ivana found herself placed in an untenable position. No longer could she ignore what was going on. If Donald had played the love game a little more skillfully, Ivana would not have had to sit there with egg all over her face. She could have continued to turn away from the problem.

Now she could no longer do so.

Breaking from the self-imposed exile of her room, she soon tracked down The Donald on the slopes—luckily he was alone—

and faced him with characteristic determination. She asked him point-blank if he was having an affair with Marla Maples.

The Donald, caught offguard, but still handling everything in that cool and professional manner he considered to be essential to the art of the deal, admitted that yes, there was someone else in his life.

Ivana blew up. It had been building to this for some months now, she knew. The air would have to be cleared. She had no idea how it was going to turn out, now. She had to have her say.

She told The Donald what she thought of him and of his womanizing. Indeed that seemed to be what he was now more interested in than in being a husband to her.

With his own low-boiling point quickly reached, Donald Trump came right back at her, professing that he had his male prerogatives as much as she had her female ones, and that he was not going to allow himself to be dictated to by a jealous wife.

And so on and so forth.

The bout lasted for several minutes, and then died out when Ivana turned away and slammed down the mountainside on her skis.

Although this argument was pretty much in the open, no one really picked up on it back in New York. But those close to both the Trumps knew that things were rapidly approaching crisis proportions.

The point of climax in the marriage of Donald and Ivana Trump had actually been reached and passed. Yet, on the surface, nothing much seemed to be happening in the ensuing several weeks. Below the surface many things were in the works.

Newsweek's coverage of the tense weeks that followed the Aspen incident include most of the salient points. The magazine's researchers learned that both the Trumps found themselves involved in an aggravated situation that required outside help of some kind. They both agreed that Michael Kennedy was to begin laying down some kind of schedule for the arrangement of an amicable divorce settlement.

As for the Trumps themselves, by the first of February they had not yet split up. But it was at the time that Donald Trump flew to Tokyo to witness a prize fight—between Mike Tyson and Buster Douglas—that the other shoe dropped.

Just as he left Trump Tower, Donald told Ivana that he would be packing up and leaving the apartment for good.

That was the first Ivana had heard that things had gone that far. And so, with Donald in the air on the way to Japan, she met with her advisers. Then she met with her friends. From these meetings a plan was formed.

But it was not until Sunday, February 11, 1990, that the plan began to unfold with the breaking of the news story about a possible collapse of the Trump marriage.

The news broke from Ivana's vantage point—not from The Donald's. It was her good friend, Liz Smith, who wrote a full-page column on the front of the *New York Daily News*, announcing that the marriage of the Trumps was on the rocks.

It was the beginning of what might be called Ivana's Week of Pain.

But Liz Smith had been forced to persuade Ivana to let her release the news. As she told it later, she had been hearing for months about the marital problems of the Trumps. Finally, she said, Ivana had admitted to her that things were coming to a head. Once she got it confirmed that a split was in the making, Liz told Ivana that she would like to handle the story.

Ivana did not want the information released at all. Liz pointed out that it was going to be released soon, once the divorce papers were filed. And, of course, Ivana knew that was true. But she persisted in her refusal.

Now Liz told Ivana that she should be represented by some kind of public relations person because she knew how things could go all wrong in the blizzard of words that would be sure to follow the breaking of such a major story. She suggested that Ivana hire John Scanlon, a public relations maven working for Daniel J. Edelman, Inc. Ivana then admitted that she and her lawyer, Michael Kennedy, had already been considering using Scanlon.

Ivana then bowed to the inevitable, and instructed Liz to go ahead with the story. Liz picked up Ivana's statement—that Donald was betraying her—to write the lead for her scoop.

In the story, Liz mentioned that Ivana had been an active partner with her husband, citing her work at Atlantic City and at the Plaza Hotel.

The fat was in the fire. From Liz Smith's scoop of the year—

of the decade, perhaps—the news snowballed into one of the greatest media circuses within memory.

Cindy Adams, scooped by Liz Smith, commented in the *New York Post*: "Donald and Ivana Trump: Wow! Do they sell papers!"

The story made only one paper on Sunday—the *Daily News*—and it was headlined "Splitsville?" Monday the *Daily News* had it: "Trump Split?" The *Post* did not wonder. "Split," it said, with a picture of the Trumps together, cut down the middle.

On Tuesday things were simmering even more. "Ivana Better Deal," said the *Daily News*, always quick to lurch into wordplay. "Over Her Dead Body," noted *Newsday*. "Gimme the Plaza!" clamored the *Post*, making Ivana out to be a latter-day Leona Helmsley.

Donald's camp tried to make the best of a bad thing, painting him as less domineering, capricious, and chauvinistically male than he seemed to be to everyone else. "He likes Ivana very much," a statement said about the separation. "But it just was not working out. For the good of all, he decided to leave."

Even the staid *New York Times* almost betrayed amusement at this reasoning and presented the following thesis in its editorial column on Valentine's Day, 1990:

"Honey, here's the deal.

"1. I swear to cherish you till death do us part. Or at least until the marriage is no longer working out.

"2. During the life of this nuptial agreement, I'll brag to the world about your achievements as a world-class skier, your qualities as a mother and your business acumen. And in fact, until the marriage is no longer working out, we will share a lot of business decisions.

"3. If, however, for any reason the marriage is no longer working out, I reserve the right to have paid spokesmen disparage your business and other abilities. I might even choose to call you arrogant.

"4. And if for any reason the marriage is no longer working out, even after many years and many millions of earnings, we'll stick strictly to this contract.

"5. This contract shall constitute the entire agreement between the parties, and no oral understanding not in writing shall be binding.

"Please sign below.

"Yours, at least for as long as the marriage is working out,

Don"

By that Wednesday other players in the story began surfacing. The *Post* pictured Donald and Marla Maples, with the headline: "Don Juan."

The media was already lined up on opposite sides of the field.

Ivana's team included Liz Smith. On her side, too, was the *Daily News*, playing the story from the standpoint of the wronged woman. On Donald's side was Cindy Adams and Suzy because, of course, they were two rivals of Liz Smith. On his side was the *Post*, because it was Cindy and Suzy's paper, and because they'd settle for Donald if Ivana was already spoken for.

The conflict began immediately.

Liz Smith was saying that Ivana walked out on Donald. "She still wants to be his wife. But the bottom line is . . . she won't give up her self-respect to do it. . . . Intimates say she had every chance to continue being Mrs. Trump by allowing her husband to live in an open marriage."

Suzy at the *Post* was saying that The Donald had taken the walk. "Get it straight," she wrote. "It's not Ivana who did the walking out. She wants to stay together at almost any price. . . . It's Donald who's breaking it up."

Irony as well as conflict seemed to dominate the Week of Pain. But it came to a head on Wednesday in an almost bizarre fashion. For months a birthday party at La Grenouille had been planned for Ivana on Valentine's Day—even though her birthday was actually February 20 and not February 14. She would be forty-one. The theme of the luncheon at the exclusive East Fifty-second Street restaurant was to be "Love of Friendship"—another irony, given the events that were swirling around her.

But there were surprises as well as tears for the beleaguered Ivana. As she stepped from her car, "beautifully turned out in a bright red dress," as Liz Smith wrote, Ivana put her head down and more or less downhilled her way into the restaurant, surrounded by bodyguards. But—surprise!—she suddenly heard cries of "Yay, Ivana! We're with you!" And that from the public.

193

Inside, she seemed stunned at the size of the crowd. Everybody was there. No one had deserted her in these, the darkest moments of her life. Her mother had flown in from Czechoslovakia, and Maria Zelnickova was present.

Even Ivana's in-laws were there in force: Mary Trump, Donald's mother, said she felt like "the villain on the premises." But she said she considered Ivana to be her daughter, rather than her in-law—because she hated the term in-law. Blaine Trump, Donald's sister, said: "I know you are going to have future birthdays that are wonderful, and we are always going to be as close as we are now."

"Nobody even mentioned Donald's name," Barbara Walters said. "It was just friendly."

"It was a happy, friendly, and supportive lunch," said author Shirley Lord. "Everybody loves Ivana."

And so it seemed, for as Ivana finally ducked out into the street to enter her car—Fifty-second Street had been closed off by the police to accommodate the crowds and the limousines—she heard cries from the crowd that were even larger than when she entered.

"Get the money, Ivana!" yelled a man.

"Twenty-five million's not enough!" a woman shouted.

And there was applause. "Take him for all he's worth!' another cried out.

By the middle of the week, everyone involved in the story was getting a bit nettled and even a mite testy in their statements about each other.

"The story was definitely leaked to [Liz Smith]," said Cindy Adams querulously. "And that left me no choice" but to side with Donald Trump. And she quoted Donald, as did all the press, when he denounced the coverage as ridiculous and totally sensationalized.

What really infuriated Donald Trump was the fact that Liz Smith had characterized Ivana Trump as a partner in his business efforts. Partner? "She's done the wallpaper in the Plaza—that's what she does!" said one spokesman.

Donald fumed some more. "That [initial story] was written by a P.R. man, and Liz went for it hook, line, and sinker. They played her like a fiddle." He was referring to John Scanlon, whom

Ivana had hired on Friday, February 9, after her discussion with Liz.

Liz snapped right back. "I don't need John Scanlon to tell me what to say!"

Other players were suiting up in the locker rooms and about to appear on the field. Donald Trump was burning the telephone wires to get his own public relations representative to launder and showcase his thoughts with the proper allure. Finally, he landed a big one: Howard J. Rubenstein, who actually was simply being let out of the closet, for he had been Trump Associates' public relations representative for years. The gods were smiling indeed, for Rubenstein represented the *New York Post* as well as The Donald—and so the teams were lining up neatly and symmetrically for the big knockdown.

In one corner:

Ivana. Liz Smith. The *New York Daily News*. John Scanlon.

And in the other corner:

The Donald. Cindy Adams. Suzy. The *New York Post*. Howard J. Rubenstein.

Now, of course, once the steamy sex matters had been attended to—with the names of half a dozen possible sex partners for The Donald—even the media got the right signals and moved on to what was really important about this marriage's collapse (if indeed it was to be a total collapse).

Money.

How much would Ivana get? $20 million? $25 million? $100 million?

By Wednesday, a discussions of the prenuptial agreement had replaced the discussions of nubile chicks and Donald in his Mandarin robe.

Prenuptial agreement.

We now come to the crux of the matter. Those of us who are not celebrities simply marry and sign the marriage certificate. But the rich and famous—they have prenuptial agreements.

The Trumps' prenuptial agreement—at least in its original form—was signed before their marriage. It was the work of none other than Roy Cohn, Donald's lawyer at the time. And it was air-tight, sealed against contamination of any kind, and bomb-proof.

Although recent years have brought the prenuptial agreement

more and more into the foreground of the marriages of celebrities, politicians, and other people with big money, they are not new at all. The modern form has its roots in the *Ketubah*, an ancient Jewish wedding contract dating back two thousand years. At the time, it was a protection for the woman in an era when women had no rights at all.

Today, according to some marriage experts, including Alexandra Leichter of Beverly Hills, "the prenuptial agreements are now used more as a weapon against the woman in many circumstances, especially in May/December weddings."

It's interesting how the language of the agreement is worded in these documents. There's the in spouse, the one with the money. That, in this case, would be Donald. Obviously, the other is the out spouse. In this case, Ivana.

Of course, once the marriage turns unhappy, and a divorce seems in the offing, the out spouse will try to set aside the agreement. If the out spouse's attorney wins, then it's an invitation to malpractice. That is, malpractice on the part of the in spouse's attorney—who the courts figure should know better.

The out spouse lawyers and the in spouse lawyers had at one another in the Trump affair in this fashion:

Donald's attorneys: "The prenuptial agreement signed by Donald and Ivana Trump is a lengthy and detailed document covering all aspects and is 100 percent enforceable in courts of law." It was not only ironclad, but steel-wrapped. That agreement was for $20 million for Ivana, custody of their three children, and the couple's home in Greenwich, Connecticut.

Ivana's attorneys: "We do not consider the so-called prenuptial agreement to be serious. It will have no relevance to a court because it is unconscionable and fraudulent." That from Michael Kennedy, Ivana's divorce lawyer.

Ivana had picked men with credits to represent her. Kennedy represented Dr. Timothy Leary, Bernadine Dohrn, Rennie Davis, Jean Harris, and the Irish Republican Army. About Ivana's case, Kennedy said: "The number of zeros here [in this case] is unfathomable to me, just beyond my comprehension."

Donald was not to be muzzled. "I've studied Michael's history. And he certainly lost lots of cases."

Donald had selected his warriors with care, too. He retained

Stanford Lotwin and Jay Goldberg. Goldberg had represented Andy Capasso, Bess Meyerson's companion, at his recent trial.

Michael Kennedy immediately attacked Howard Rubenstein Associates, Donald's public relations representatives for "leaking comments from Mr. Trump that criticized Mrs. Trump's professional competence and likened her to Leona Helmsley." In a letter to Rubenstein, he wrote: "Publicity agents from your agency purportedly speaking for Donald Trump have been slandering Mrs. Trump."

Donald's cohorts regrouped. Cindy Adams quoted Jay Goldberg in a column as saying:

"I'm a killer. I can rip skin off a body. Once I was to cross-examine a guy in a real-estate deal and, before I was hired, the people told me, 'We want you to cause him physical pain on the stand.' I said, 'Sure, Okay, I can do that.' And I did."

Kennedy lobbed that one right back at Donald's side. He claimed that Ivana considered the Goldberg statement as a threat against her and her children. He said he had ordered him "to have no further negotiations nor anything else to do with you."

Goldberg came back immediately with a response. He suggested that Kennedy was something of a fool "because of his willingness to accept an inaccurate comment, which on its face does not even purport to contain a reference to this case."

Bingo!

Had Goldberg said what he was quoted by Cindy Adams as having said?

"I don't justify a column of Cindy Adams. That's not my business."

Cindy Adams commented: "He [Goldberg] did not say that he is going to tear the skin off Ivana. He was just boasting."

The Donald surfaced. He said that he was "very angry at the statement—until he [Goldberg] told me he never said it." He stated that he would never allow a statement like that to be made by his lawyer.

As the week wore on, with charges thrown back and forth about Ivana's competence or incompetence in her jobs, it became quite obvious to her that her job at the Plaza Hotel was in deep jeopardy.

At the start of the week, it had been rumored that Donald would fire her that very day as president of the Plaza. In fact, when Ivana arrived, she found her office locked. Later in the day the rumor went out that her status was uncertain. But by then she had been let in and was hard at work.

"Donald would not do anything to hurt her right now, and, anyway, he hasn't made up his mind as to what her role at the Plaza will be," said Dan Klores soothingly. One of The Donald's spokesmen, Klores was apparently cast as the good guy among a pride of bad guys.

"This is an extremely difficult time for Mrs. Trump and her children," Kennedy shot back for the Ivana camp. "She is a family woman. Her marriage and her family have always been the most important things in her life. Mr. Trump has now left her and her children, and while one hopes for a reconciliation, my mandate at this time is to document . . . the years of marriage and partnership in the Trump holdings."

Donald himself got into the act.

"Ivana doesn't want the money," he told a columnist with magnanimous humility. "She wants Donald. She totally loves me."

Later on he assumed a more wistful attitude, and said publicly: "We just grew apart. I think Ivana is a fabulous woman, but sometimes people change and go on different paths." His pre-nuptial agreement was ironclad—"a sacred document" in his words, "bound in stone." But he might "go a step further, because I happen to love Ivana, that's a decision that I will make. A settlement for $100 million, maybe? More? No one could be sure.

He even said that Ivana had done a good job at the Plaza. He would let her stay on, if she wanted to. "It's something that I think I would honor. She likes running the hotel. It gives her something to do."

It was now evident that the remarks about a dollar a year and all the clothes she can buy were decidedly apropos. Ivana, from Donald's point of view, was being allowed to work only because it gave her something to do.

Indeed, had Ivana opted for a salary early on—insisted on it— she might not have found herself in the ridiculous position she was now in.

On Friday of the Week of Pain, the *New York Post* came up with a mean-spirited layout and headline for the front page. The story actually concerned a quote from two alleged friends of Marla Maples, to the effect that she had told them that she had enjoyed probably the "best sex I've ever had" with Donald Trump. Somebody had to dig for that.

But look what the *Post* editors did. They silhouetted a huge picture of Donald Trump's face smiling broadly, with a look of lechery in his eyes. The big headline beside this enormous portrait jumped out at you:

"BEST SEX I'VE EVER HAD"

The obvious reading was that Donald was saying the words, speaking about Marla. At the top of the page, a tiny subhead read: "Marla boasts to her pals about Donald."

The implication of the cover was blatant. Ivana was no good. Marla was the best. Donald said so.

No wonder that when Ivana was showed the front page she burst into tears and was inconsolable. "Things can't get any worse than they are now!" she sobbed to friends.

And it was no wonder that on that same day, she met with Cardinal John O'Connor in his office. "It was a private meeting," the archdiocesan spokesman said, declining to say what was discussed.

For Ivana to meet with Cardinal O'Connor was no surprise, of course. As a Roman Catholic, she had made no effort to accompany her husband to his church—when he went—and now that she found herself besieged by personal troubles it was only natural that she turn to the familiar for succor and support.

Cardinal O'Connor also refused to say what he and Ivana had talked about, but he did point out what he usually said to other couples in the situation in which the Trumps found themselves.

"I try to help them to think together, talk together, pray together, permit some outsider to try to look more objectively at their situation than frequently they can look at it. These are very general things applicable to all couples."

Ivana's father, Milos Zelnicek, flew in from Czechoslovakia to be by his daughter's side. Her mother, of course, had arrived earlier to be present for Ivana's Valentine's Day birthday party.

The Donald was realistic about how his public image would suffer from the news of the impending divorce. "I know at first the sympathy goes to the woman, and it should. She's good people." He said that he would treat her right. "It's going to be amicable, I promise you that. Listen, we never had a fight. The kids never saw anything wrong, and they're going to be great. She's going to be great."

Was it Ivana or Donald the public fancied?

"I think long ago Donald had a goal and wanted a certain kind of woman," *People* magazine quoted one of Ivana's acquaintances in Palm Beach. "He likes flash. She sets him off. You don't miss her in a crowd."

"Ivana came from this European tradition," observed interior designer Mario Buatta. "She came to America, where the streets are supposed to be paved in gold. She worked hard to get that dream. She worked her ass off, and she was finally getting credit for that work, and she gets slapped in the face like this. Donald Trump has a monster ego."

Another observer agreed. "Success is what really turned him against her. Donald is not doing anything for love. This is not about him having affairs. This is about two egos wearing away at each other. The more she worked at what she thought he'd like, the less he liked it."

James Revson, the *Newsday* columnist, wrote: "There is enormous sympathy for her. You couldn't measure with an eyedropper the sympathy for him in this town."

"He is a very cold man," the Palm Beach friend said. "He figures everyone in terms of how he can buy or sell them."

"He's a fool," said Mai Hallingby. "Ivana has supported Donald 100 percent in everything he's done. It's going to be difficult for him to find another wife like that."

In a subtle way, a great deal had happened within one week— this bizarre, memorable Week of Pain. At its end, Donald Trump, billionaire, builder of monuments to himself, wheeler and dealer, maker of fortunes, breaker of competitors, this man of stature and dominance . . . Donald Trump had shrunken incredibly. The small boy that had never grown up within him seemed to have taken over the external persona of The Donald— The Donald that Ivana had loved and cherished and so foolishly trusted.

He appeared quite like the little boy who got caught with his hand in the cookie jar. Pictures of him staring blankly into cameras shooting him again and again showed a look of concern and self-pity, as if he had no idea why anyone would want to stare at him, or, certainly, choose to blame him for any of the cookies he had eaten.

"I thought it would be a one-day wonder," he said abstractedly. Instead of that. . . .

The little boy seemed about to burst into tears.

As for Ivana, even though she kept her head down when she ran the gauntlet of the media liens, she was erect and the epitome of courage. Not for her the sudden disappearing act—as the other woman had effected, with the aid of The Donald. Every day Ivana had gone to work in the midst of chaos, vituperation, and outright scorn. She had done what she had to do, with her head at least figuratively high, and her integrity intact.

Somehow the duo had changed places. Out of the change, Ivana was now the leader, the strong one, the dominant partner.

And The Donald, to put it mildly, was reduced.

The final irony of the Week of Pain—a lesser one than the irony of Ivana's Valentine's birthday party in the midst of the matrimonial scuffle of the decade—occurred on Friday, too.

For many weeks Ivana and Donald Trump had been scheduled for a photographic session at Richard Avedon's in New York. The reason for the posing was that Revlon had selected the Trumps to initiate an ongoing campaign to advertise its cosmetics. The campaign was to feature a series of women that Revlon was going to call "Unforgettable Women." Ivana was to be Number One.

Sadly, during the fracas in the press and on the airwaves, Revlon's representatives called Ivana's office and said that the Richard Avedon shoot for February 16 was going to be canceled.

And yet—who could ever say that Ivana was not the epitome and paradigm of the Unforgettable Woman?